Carrying on in Key Stage 1

# Sand

Published 2011 by A&C Black Publishers Limited
36 Soho Square, London W1D 3QY

**www.acblack.com**

ISBN 978-1-4081-3973-8

First published 2008 by Featherstone Education Ltd

Text © Ros Bayley, Lyn Broadbent, Sally Featherstone 2008

Photographs © Fotolia 2011, Shutterstock 2011

Additional photos © Lynn Broadbent, Ros Bayley, Sally Featherstone, Sarah
Featherstone 2008, ASCO

Designed by Lynda Murray

A CIP record for this publication is available from the British Library.

Printed in Malta by Gutenburg Press Ltd

This book is produced using paper that is made from wood grown in managed,
sustainable forests. It is natural, renewable and recyclable.

The logging and manufacturing processes conform to the environmental
regulations of the country of origin.

To see our full range of titles visit **www.acblack.com**

# Contents

# Introduction

This series of books is intended to support the continuing growth and development of independent learning and practical activities, which are key features of the Early Years Foundation Stage (EYFS).

Children in Key Stage 1 need and deserve the chance to build on the best of practice in the EYFS, which carefully balances adult directed tasks with learning that children initiate and develop themselves, often in the company of responsive adults. These activities, which include sand and water play, construction, role play, independent mark making and writing, creative work, dance and movement, and outdoor play, are some of the activities children value most and miss most in Years 1 and 2.

What's it like in year 1?

There en't no sand and the work's too 'ard.

This quote from a Year 1 boy echoes the feelings of many children who need a continuation of the learning styles and situations offered in Reception classes. However, many teachers in Key Stage One feel intense pressure to concentrate on activities that require recording and increasing levels of direction from adults. Why is this, and is it right for teachers to feel so pressured?

One thing we know from research is that practical activity and independent learning are essential for brain growth and reinforcement of growing abilities throughout childhood, at least until the onset of puberty, and for many children this is a lifelong need. We also know that the embedding of learning and the transformation of this into real understanding takes time and practice. Skills need to be reinforced by revisiting them in many different contexts in child-initiated learning and practical

challenges. Practical tasks in real life situations will be far more effective than rote learning, worksheets or adult direction.

It is also clear from brain research that many boys (and some girls) are just not ready by the end of Reception to embark on a formal curriculum which involves a lot of sitting down, listening and writing. Their bodies and their brains still need action, challenge and freedom to explore materials and resources.

But this does not mean that challenge should be absent from such activity! The brain feeds on challenge and novelty, so teachers and other adults working in Key Stage One need to structure the experiences, so they build on existing skills and previous activities, while presenting opportunities to explore familiar materials in new and exciting ways. Such challenges and activities can:

- be led by the Programme of Study for Key Stage 1
- focus on thinking skills and personal capabilities
- relate to real world situations and stimuli
- help children to achieve the five outcomes for Every Child Matters.

'I hear and I forget,
I see and I remember,
I do and I understand.'
*Ancient Chinese Proverb*

## Every Child Matters

The five outcomes:

- Enjoy and achieve
- Stay safe
- Be healthy
- Make a positive contribution
- Achieve economic well-being

In **Carrying on in Key Stage 1**, we aim to give you the rationale, the process and the confidence to continue a practical, child-centred curriculum which also helps you as teachers to meet the requirements of the statutory curriculum for Key Stage One. Each book in the series follows the same format, and addresses objectives from many areas of the National Curriculum. Of course, when children work on practical challenges, curriculum elements become intertwined, and many will be going on simultaneously.

## The role of the adult

Of course, even during child-initiated learning, the role of the adult is crucial. Sensitive adults play many roles as they support, challenge and engage the children in their care. High quality teaching is not easy! If teachers want to expand experiences and enhance learning, they need to be able to stand back, to work alongside, and to extend or scaffold the children's learning by offering provocations and challenges to their thinking. The diagram on the right attempts to describe this complex task, and the way that adults move around the elements in the circle of learning. For ease of reading we have described the elements in the following way, and each double page spread covers all three of the vital roles adults play.

### Previous experience: recognising and building on the practical activities which children have experienced before

This element of the process is vital in scaffolding children's learning so it makes sense to them. Your knowledge of the Foundation Stage curriculum and the way it is organised will be vital in knowing where to start.
Teachers and other adults should have first hand knowledge of both the resources and the activities which have been available and how they have been offered in both child-initiated and adult-led activities. This knowledge should be gained by visiting the Reception classes in action, and by talking to adults and children as they work. Looking at Reception planning will also help.

### The responsive adult: Understanding the range of adult roles, and the effect different roles have on children's learning

Responsive adults react in different ways to what they see and hear during the day. This knowledge will influence the way they plan for further experiences to meet emerging needs and build on individual interests. The diagram illustrates the complex and interlinking ways in which adults interact with children's learning. Observing, co-playing and extending learning often happen simultaneously, flexibly and sometimes unconsciously. It is only when we reflect on our work with children that we realise what a complex and skilled activity is going on.

### Offering challenges and provocations

As the adults collect information about the learning, they begin to see how they can help children to extend and scaffold their thinking and learning. The adults offer challenges or provocations which act like grit in an oyster, provoking the children to produce responses and think in new ways about what they know and can do.

### Linking the learning with the skills and content of the curriculum

As the children grapple with new concepts and skills, adults can make direct links with curriculum intentions and content. These links can be mapped out across the range of knowledge, skills and understanding contained in the curriculum guidance for Key Stage One. It is also possible to map the development of thinking skills, personal capabilities and concepts which link the taught curriculum with the real world.

**The adult as extender of learning**
- discusses ideas
- shares thinking
- makes new possibilities evident
- instigates new opportunities for learning
- extends and builds on learning and interests
- supports children in making links in learning
- models new skills and techniques

**The adult as co-player**
- shares responsibility with the child
- offers suggestions
- asks open questions
- responds sensitively
- models and imitates
- plays alongside

**The adult as observer**
- listens attentively
- observes carefully
- records professionally
- interprets skilfully

As children plan, explore, invent, extend, construct, discuss, question and predict in the rich experiences planned and offered, they will communicate what they are learning through speech and actions, as well as through the outcomes of activities.

## Looking for the learning

Assessment for learning involves adults and children in sharing and analysing what they discover. Reflecting on learning, through discussion with other children and adults, is a key factor in securing skills and abilities, fixing and 'hard wiring' the learning in each child's brain. And, of course, teachers and other adults need to recognise, confirm and record children's achievements, both for the self esteem this brings to the children and to fulfil their own duties as educators.

You could find out what children already know and have experienced by:

- talking to them as individuals and in small groups

- talking to parents and other adults who know them well (teaching assistants are often wonderful sources of information about individual children)

- visiting the Reception classes and looking at spaces, storage and access to resources, including the use of these out of doors

- providing free access to materials and equipment and watching how children use them when you are not giving any guidance

- talking as a group or class about what children already know about the materials and those they particularly enjoy using.

### Using the curriculum grid to observe, to recognise learning and celebrate achievement

At the end of this section you will find a photocopiable curriculum grid covering the whole Programme of Study for Key Stage 1 which can be used for planning and particularly for recording observations. This is a 'shorthand version' of the full grid included at the end of the book on pages 40-48.

We suggest that as the children work on the provocations and other challenges in this book, adults (teachers and teaching assistants) can use the grid to observe groups of children and record the areas of the curriculum they are covering in their work. The grid can also be used to record what children say and describe in plenary sessions and other discussions.

These observations will enable you to recognise the learning that happens as children explore the materials and engage with the challenging questions you ask and the problems you pose. And of course, as you observe, you will begin to see what needs to happen next; identifying the next steps in learning! This logical and vital stage in the process may identify:

- some children who will be ready for more of the same activity

- some who need to repeat and reinforce previous stages

- some who need to relate skills to new contexts, the same activity or skill practised in a new place or situation

- some who will want to extend or sustain the current activity in time, space or detail

- others who will wish to record their work in photos, drawings, models, stories, video and so on.

The grid also identifies the key skills which children need for thinking about and evaluating their work. Many schools now observe and evaluate how well these skills are developing when children work on challenging projects and investigations.

## Ready for more?

Offering extension activities is a way of scaffolding children's learning, taking the known into the unknown, the familiar into the new, the secure into the challenging. It is the role of the adult to turn their knowledge of the children into worthwhile, long-term lines of enquiry and development which will become self-sustaining and last throughout life.

At the end of each section in the book you will find a selection of useful resources, links and other information to help you support children in making structures, sculptures and other 3D creations. You could use these resources by encouraging individuals and groups:

- to use the Internet to find images and information

- to use ICT equipment such as cameras, tape recorders, video and dictaphones to record their explorations and experiments

- to explore information books in libraries and other places at home and at school

- to make contact by email and letter with experts, craftsmen, artists, manufacturers, suppliers and other contacts

- to make books, films, PowerPoint presentations

- to record their work in photographs and other media

- to respond to stimuli such as photographs, video, exhibitions and other creative stimuli

- to look at the built and natural environment with curiosity, interest and creativity

- to become involved in preserving the natural world, develop environmental awareness and support recycling

- to look at the world of work and extend their ideas of what they might become and how they might live their lives

- to develop a sense of economic awareness and the world of work in its widest sense

- to feel a sense of community and to explore how they might make a contribution to the school and wider communities in which they live

- to work together and develop the ability to think, reason and solve problems in their learning.

The suggested resources include websites, books, contacts and addresses. There are also some photographs which may inspire young learners as they work on the provocations and challenges suggested.

We hope you will find the ideas in this book useful in stimulating your work with children in Year 1 and Year 2. Before trying the activities please check for allergies and be aware of safety at all times. The ideas, photos and provocations we have included are only a start to your thinking and exploring together. Of course you and the children will have many more as you start to expand the work they do in these practical areas, providing a rich curriculum base using familiar and well loved materiaals.

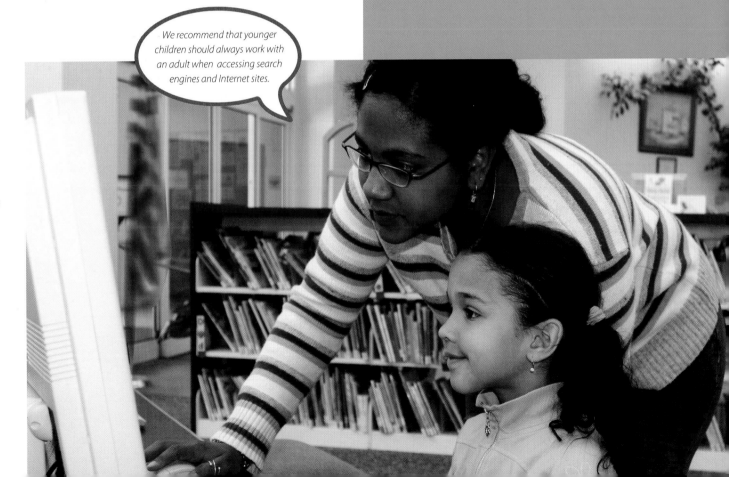

*We recommend that younger children should always work with an adult when accessing search engines and Internet sites.*

# Planning and observation of _____ (the activity)   Name: _____   Date: _____

## Literacy

| Lit 1 Speak | Lit 2 Listen | Lit 3 Group | Lit 4 Drama | Lit 5 Word | Lit 6 Spell | Lit 7 Text 1 | Lit 8 Text 2 | Lit 9 Text 3 | Lit 10 Text 4 | Lit 11 Sentence | Lit 12 Presentation |
|---|---|---|---|---|---|---|---|---|---|---|---|
| 1.1 | 2.1 | 3.1 | 4.1 | 5.1 | 6.1 | 7.1 | 8.1 | 9.1 | 10.1 | 11.1 | 12.1 |
| 1.2 | 2.2 | 3.2 | 4.2 | 5.2 | 6.2 | 7.2 | 8.2 | 9.2 | 10.2 | 11.2 | 12.2 |

## Numeracy

| Num 1 U&A | Num 2 Count | Num 3 Number | Num 4 Calculate | Num 5 Shape | Num 6 Measure | Num 7 Data |
|---|---|---|---|---|---|---|
| 1.1 | 2.1 | 3.1 | 4.1 | 5.1 | 6.1 | 7.1 |
| 1.2 | 2.2 | 3.2 | 4.2 | 5.2 | 6.2 | 7.2 |

## Science

| SC1 Enquiry | | | SC2 Life processes | | | | | SC3 Materials | | SC4 Physical processes | | |
|---|---|---|---|---|---|---|---|---|---|---|---|---|
| Sc 1.1 | Sc 1.2 | Sc 1.3 | Sc 2.1 | Sc 2.2 | Sc 2.3 | Sc 2.4 | Sc 2.5 | Sc 3.1 | Sc 3.2 | Sc 4.1 | Sc4.2 | Sc 4.3 |
| 1.1a | 1.2a | 1.3a | 2.1a | 2.2a | 2.3a | 2.4a | 2,5a | 3.1a | 3.2a | 4.1a | 4.2a | 4.3a |
| 1.1b | 1.2b | 1.3b | 2.1b | 2.2b | 2.3b | 2.4b | 2,5b | 3.1b | 3.2b | 4.1b | 4.2b | 4.3b |
| 1.1c | 1.2c | 1.3c | 2.1c | 2.2c | 2.3c |  | 2,5c | 3.1c |  | 4.1c | 4.2c | 4.3c |
| 1.1d |  |  |  | 2.2d |  |  |  | 3.1d |  |  |  | 4.3d |
|  |  |  |  | 2.2e |  |  |  |  |  |  |  |  |
|  |  |  |  | 2.2f |  |  |  |  |  |  |  |  |
|  |  |  |  | 2.2g |  |  |  |  |  |  |  |  |

## History

| H1 Chronology | H2 Events, people | H3 Interpret | H4 Enquire | H5 Org and comm | H6 Breadth |
|---|---|---|---|---|---|
| 1a | 2a | 3a | 4a | 5a | 6a |
| 1b | 2b |  | 4b |  | 6b |
|  |  |  |  | 6c |  |
|  |  |  |  | 6d |  |

## Geography

| G1.1 and Enquiry | G1.2 | G2 Places | G3 Processes | G4 Environment | G5 Breadth |
|---|---|---|---|---|---|
| 1.1a | 1.2a | 2a | 3a | 4a | 5a |
| 1.1b | 1.2b | 2b | 3b | 4b | 5b |
| 1.1c | 1.2c | 2c |  |  | 5c |
| 1.1d | 1.2d | 2d |  |  | 5d |
|  |  | 2e |  |  |  |

## Notes on how to take the learning forward

## Music

| M1<br>Performing | M2<br>Composing | M3<br>Appraising | M4<br>Listening | M5<br>Breadth |
|---|---|---|---|---|
| 1a | 2a | 3a | 4a | 5a |
| 1b | 2b | 3b | 4b | 5b |
| 1c | | | 4c | 5c |
| | | | 5d | |

## Art and Design

| A&D 1<br>Ideas | A&D 2<br>Making | A&D 3<br>Evaluating | A&D 4<br>Materials | A&D 5<br>Breadth |
|---|---|---|---|---|
| 1a | 2a | 3a | 4a | 5a |
| 1b | 2b | 3b | 4b | 5b |
| | 2c | | 4c | 5c |
| | | | | 5d |

## Design and Technology

| D&T 1<br>Developing | D&T 2<br>Tool use | D&T 3<br>Evaluating | D&T 4<br>Materials | D&T 5<br>Breadth |
|---|---|---|---|---|
| 1a | 2a | 3a | 4a | 5a |
| 1b | 2b | 3b | 4b | 5b |
| 1c | 2c | | | 5c |
| 1d | 2d | | | |
| 1e | 2e | | | |

## PSHE

| PSHE1<br>Confidence and respect | PSHE2<br>Citizenship | PSHE3<br>Health | PSHE4<br>Relationships |
|---|---|---|---|
| 1a | 2a | 3a | 4a |
| 1b | 2b | 3b | 4b |
| 1c | 2c | 3c | 4c |
| 1d | 2d | 3d | 4d |
| 1e | 2e | 3e | 4e |
| | 2f | 3f | |
| | 2g | 3g | |
| | 2h | | |

## ICT

| ICT 1<br>Finding out | | ICT2<br>Ideas | ICT3<br>Reviewing | ICT4<br>Breadth |
|---|---|---|---|---|
| 1.1a | 1.2a | 2a | 3a | 4a |
| 1.1b | 1.2b | 2b | 3b | 4b |
| 1.1c | 1.2c | 2c | 3c | 4c |
| | 1.2d | | | |

## PE

| PE 1<br>Develop skills | PE 2<br>Apply skills | PE 3<br>Evaluate | PE 4<br>Fitness | PE 5<br>Breadth |
|---|---|---|---|---|
| 1a | 2a | 3a | 4a | 5a dance |
| 1b | 2b | 3b | 4b | 5b games |
| | 2c | 3c | | 5c gym |

| Critical skills | Thinking skills |
|---|---|
| problem solving | observing |
| decision making | classifying |
| critical thinking | prediction |
| creative thinking | making inferences |
| communication | problem solving |
| organisation | drawing conclusions |
| management | |
| leadership | |

# Funnels, tubes and scoops

### Previous experience

Children will have had experience of simple scoops and funnels in the Foundation Stage and even before. They are classic sand tools for:

- free play in sand trays and boxes indoors and in the garden
- scooping sand into containers
- lifting sand and letting it fall, exploring how it moves
- filling and emptying diggers and boats
- filling bottles and other containers with narrow necks
- ladling sand into paper or plastic bags in role-play, as 'food' or 'shopping'
- carrying sand around in buckets and barrows.

## The responsive adult

In the early stages of working with these materials it is crucial to continue to observe the children. Only by doing this can you set developmentally appropriate challenges and provocations. The ideas listed here are offered as suggestions; the most exciting challenges will arise from children's own interests and motivations, which will only become apparent as you spend time with them, watching and joining them in their play. As you do this, you will be moving between the three interconnecting roles of observer, co-player, extender described below, and will be able to decide what you need to do next to take the learning forward. In three interconnecting roles, the responsive adult will be:

### Observer

- observing
- listening
- interpreting

### Co-player

- modelling
- playing alongside
- offering suggestions
- responding sensitively
- initiating with care!

### Extender

- discussing ideas
- sharing thinking
- modelling new skills
- asking open questions
- being an informed extender
- instigating ideas and thoughts
- supporting children as they make links in learning
- making possibilities evident
- introducing new ideas and resources
- offering challenges and provocations

## Offering challenges and provocations

As children get older they can manage much smaller versions of the tools they have been using in the Foundation Stage. Search in bargain shops, cook shops, and garden centres for small versions of scoops, funnels, measuring spoons, and look for smaller containers to pour and scoop into. Add some small bottles, funnels and tubing, and this activity will help to refine fine motor skills for writing and 3D vision for reading.

- Find a way to tell which scoop holds the most sand. How did you do it?

- Use the biggest scoop to fill the biggest container. How many scoops did it need? Now use the biggest scoop and the smallest container. How many did it need? Try the smallest scoop and the biggest container.

- Fix one of the funnels into the end of one of the tubes. Now see how well it works. Try other combinations of tubes, funnels and scoops to find out which ones work best with different containers.

- Can you find a way of suspending a funnel and tube so you don't have to hold it while you pour in the sand? How did you do it?

- Experiment with dry and damp sand. Which works best with the scoops? ... with the tubes? ... with the funnels? Why do you think this is?

- Find a way of testing all the scoops so you can find out which one holds most sand. How did you do it? Were there any surprises?

- Look at some recycled bottles and other containers. Can you make your own scoops from these? Try some bottles with handles (from milk or juice) and make these into scoops by cutting away the bits of the bottle that you don't need. Take care with cutting tools!

- Find a really big container and fill it with sand, using your scoops. Can you find out how heavy the container is?

## Ready for more?

- Set up a challenge with your friends. Agree on a container and a scoop or spoon. Now each one guesses how many scoops will fill the container. Record the guesses, and then measure. Who was nearest? Try again with a different container.

- Use scoops, funnels and tubing to transfer the sand from one sand box to another without touching the sand. How did you do it? Try with wet and dry sand — which is easiest?

- Can you use scoops and funnels to make a sand wheel work? Could you design a different sand machine, and make it with boxes, tubes and glue?

- Dry sand goes through tubes and funnels more easily than damp sand. How can you turn damp sand into dry sand? Do some experiments with your ideas and record what you find out in photos or on a chart.

- Find some construction gears, straws or other pieces to make sand machines with scoops on them. Use the machines to shift the sand or load lorries and trucks.

- Look at the big sand pit machine on this page. How does the sand get up the conveyor belt? Could you make a machine to lift sand up so you can make piles or load toy lorries?

# Materials, websites, books and other references

## Materials

For beach and sand toys including diggers and shovels and a ride on digger: **www.growingtreetoys.com**

ASCO Educational; suppliers of equipment and tools for sand play: **www.ascoeducational.co.uk** for sand trays, scoops and tools.

Other education suppliers will have more equipment, try:

Eduzone: **www.eduzone.co.uk**

Hope: **www.hope-education.co.uk**

Early Learning Centre: **www.elc.co.uk**

TTS Group have a wide range of diggers and other sand toys: **www.tts-group.co.uk**

Get silver sand from an educational supplier or garden centre — builder's sand is very gritty and sometimes stains hands and clothes. Bags of gravel and pebbles from garden centres are a cheap way of extending resources for digging and scooping.

## Google images

For images of scooping and pouring try:

- digger
- scoop
- sand
- seaside
- sandcastle
- sand wheel.

## Ideas

Try The Building Centre **www.buildingcentre.org.uk** go to 'links/education' and find the school of architecture nearest to you. They might be interested in working with the children on a project using some of the ideas in this book!

## Books

Some suitable books for younger readers include:

**Sand and Water Play**: Simple, Creative Activities for Young Children; Sherrie West; Gryphon House

**The Little Book of Sand and Water**; Sally Featherstone; A&C Black

**Sand and Soil (Rocks, Minerals, and Resources)**; Beth Gurney; Crabtree Publishing

**Wild About Trucks and Diggers**; Caroline Bingham; Ticktock media.

# Sieves, jugs and containers

## Previous experience

These tools are also familiar in most Foundation Stage settings. Children will have used them:

- during free play indoors and out of doors
- in cooking activities for sieving lumps from flour or icing sugar
- for straining pasta, vegetables and other foods cooked in water
- with gloop, flour, seeds, dried pulses, foam and other malleable materials
- in sand trays and builders' trays
- for sieving small objects out of sand or water
- in the garden to sieve and sort soil, compost or other natural materials
- in domestic role-play, cooking and making other food in role.

## The responsive adult

In the early stages of working with these materials it is crucial to continue to observe the children. Only by doing this can you set developmentally appropriate challenges and provocations. The ideas listed here are offered as suggestions; the most exciting challenges will arise from children's own interests and motivations, which will only become apparent as you spend time with them, watching and joining them in their play. As you do this, you will be moving between the three interconnecting roles of observer, co-player, extender described below, and will be able to decide what you need to do next to take the learning forward. In three interconnecting roles, the responsive adult will be:

### Observer

- observing
- listening
- interpreting

### Co-player

- modelling
- playing alongside
- offering suggestions
- responding sensitively
- initiating with care!

### Extender

- discussing ideas
- sharing thinking
- modelling new skills
- asking open questions
- being an informed extender
- instigating ideas and thoughts
- supporting children as they make links in learning
- making possibilities evident
- introducing new ideas and resources
- offering challenges and provocations

## Offering challenges and provocations

Small versions of sieves, whisks, containers, bowls, colanders etc can be found in cook shops, toyshops, bargain shops and DIY stores. Collect as many different sorts and sizes as you can. Using them will help with motor skills in writing and reading.

- Use the sieves to explore sand, sawdust, gravel and soil. How do sieves work? What do they do?

- Add some grains of rice to dry sand. How can you use the sieves and colanders to get the rice grains out of the sand? Which one works best?

- Hold up a sieve or colander full of sand and watch carefully how the sand falls through the holes. What do you see? Why do you think it happens?

- Fill a jug with sand and pour it slowly into a sieve. Can your friend take a photo of what happens? Make a label for the photo and put it where other children can see it.

- Mix some dry sand and some sequins. Now add water till the sand is completely under water. What happens to the sequins? Can you catch them? What could you use?

- Mix some small toys in the dry sand. What is the best way to get them out again without touching the sand?

- Use a sieve or colander to fill a big bowl with sand. What happens? Is it the best tool to use? What would be a better tool?

- Mix some rice, sand, lentils and dried peas. Now try to sort them out again using the sieves and colanders. Is this easy? How can you do it?

- Find a big piece of paper and a colander or sieve. Now hold the colander or sieve over the paper and pour some sand through it. Watch what the sand does as it falls on the paper. Take photos of the way sand falls through colanders and sieves with different sized holes or patterns. Try pouring slowly or very fast and watch what happens.

## Ready for more?

- Get some soil or compost. Mix it with water in a bowl or bucket until it is very wet. Now use the sieves to strain the watery mixture. What do you catch? What stays in the water? Why do some of the bits stay in the water? How could you get them out?

- Line a colander or sieve with paper towels and try this with a watery mixture of sand or compost. What happens?

- Does a sieve work if you turn it upside down? What do you find out when you try? Why do you think this happens?

- Get some flour or icing sugar and tip it into a sieve. Shake the sieve. What happens? What is left in the sieve. Why do chefs sieve flour and icing sugar? Try shaking icing sugar or flour on to black paper. Can you make patterns?

- Roll out some dough or plasticene. Press a colander or sieve into the surface and look at what happens. Look inside the sieve and at the dough.

- Look at the pictures of a sieves on this page. Maybe you could borrow a garden sieve from someone who likes gardening. What is this sieve used for? How is it different from a kitchen sieve? Try it with some soil or compost.

- Pour water slowly through a small sieve or colander onto a thin layer of dry sand. What happens? Look at the patterns.

# Materials, websites, books and other references

## Materials

Suppliers of plastic containers, sieves and other sand toys:

ASCO www.ascoeducational.co.uk for general sand equipment.

TTS Group www.tts-group.co.uk for sieves and funnels and builder's trays.

You can also get builder's tray (cement mixing trays) from DIY superstores such as B&Q, Wilkinsons or Homebase. Garden sieves are cheap and durable. Get some cat litter trays or square washing up bowls from a Bargain Shop for space saving sand play.

Buy some big plastic plant saucers, windowsill plant trays or shallow planters from a garden centre for individual play on tables.

Send for some cookware catalogues such as Lakeland Plastics www.lakeland.co.uk

Buy lentils, dried peas and beans and dry pasta in bulk from supermarkets or Asian/Italian wholesalers. You could ask your local shopkeepers (and the parents) for 'past the sell by date' pasta and pulses to make this activity more eco-friendly.

## Google images

For useful images of sand play and equipment enter the name or type of the tool or activity you want to see e.g.

- sieve
- colander
- sifter
- strainer

for hundreds of different sorts.

## Websites

Google cooking equipment for lots of sites.

## Books

Some suitable books for younger readers include:

The Riddle of the Stolen Sand (a junior detective story); George Edward Stanley; Aladdin

The Sand Tray (Thinkers); Don Rowe; A&C Black

Sand and Soil (Rocks, Minerals, and Resources); Beth Gurney; Crabtree Publishing

Sand on the Move (First Books--Earth & Sky Science); Roy Gallant; Franklin Watts

Dazzling Diggers; Tody Mitton; Kingfisher Books

Diggers and Cranes; Jim Pipe; Franklin Watts.

# Small world

## Previous experience

By the time children leave the Foundation Stage they should have had extensive experience of constructing small worlds:

- in free play indoors and out of doors
- in role-play situations
- in play with builders' trays and story boxes
- in exploring ways of making steady structures
- when playing with train sets and play mats
- in sand and water play
- when playing with clay, dough, malleable materials.

They will also have had experience of:

- developing narratives and constructing scenarios
- using fine motor skills to place objects.

## The responsive adult

In the early stages of working with these materials it is crucial to continue to observe the children. Only by doing this can you set developmentally appropriate challenges and provocations. The ideas listed here are offered as suggestions; the most exciting challenges will arise from children's own interests and motivations, which will only become apparent as you spend time with them, watching and joining them in their play. As you do this, you will be moving between the three interconnecting roles of observer, co-player, extender described below, and will be able to decide what you need to do next to take the learning forward. In three interconnecting roles, the responsive adult will be:

### Observer

- observing
- listening
- interpreting

### Co-player

- modelling
- playing alongside
- offering suggestions
- responding sensitively
- initiating with care!

### Extender

- discussing ideas
- sharing thinking
- modelling new skills
- asking open questions
- being an informed extender
- instigating ideas and thoughts
- supporting children as they make links in learning
- making possibilities evident
- introducing new ideas and resources
- offering challenges and provocations

## Offering challenges and provocations

Children may need practice in accepting and carrying out challenges presented by adults, when they have been used to free play in sand. You may need to introduce this gradually and sit with the children as they work to encourage them to stay on task.

- Can you make a plan or a list of the materials you need to make a jungle in the sand? Collect the things you need and build the jungle according to your plan.

- Can you build a space station for astronauts? A farm for some animals? A desert island, a town or a village?

- Look on Google Images 'jungle' or 'rainforest' and use the pictures to help you build a scene.

- Write a jungle story and then make some scenes to photograph for the illustrations.

- Use books to help you find out about animals, birds and plants that live in rainforests and jungles. Use the information to help you with your project.

- Read a jungle story and make some scenes of different parts of the story. Photograph your scenes. Add some play people and make a jungle diary for the explorers.

- Watch *Jungle Book*, *Finding Nemo*, *Charlotte's Web* or another favourite film, and make a replica of your favourite scene from the film, complete with animals and people.

- When you are at home or outside, look for objects that you could use for your small world scenes — leaves, twigs, stones, bark, seeds, nuts and acorns. Use these to make your own stories by adding small people or animals.

- Use small boxes or cartons to make buildings for your scenes, or find some small blocks of wood that you can make into buildings by drawing windows and doors on the surfaces.

- Make a small world version of your house or your bedroom with furniture, people and other objects.

## Ready for more?

◆ Read *Where the Forest Meets the Sea*. Collect some twigs, shells, stones, branches to make replicas of some of the scenes in the story.

◆ Visit a garden centre and find pot plants that grow in jungles and rainforests. Buy some small ones to add to your scenes. Photograph your jungles.

◆ Mix some sand with compost and plant some seeds to make your jungle even more realistic. Try grass seed, mustard and cress, or rocket. Remember to keep the seeds moist by spraying them with a hand sprayer.

◆ Now use the skills you have as jungle designers to make other sorts of landscapes — mountains, islands, forests, arctic lands, rivers and streams. Use books and the internet to find information. Photograph your creations and make an exhibition or a book.

◆ Make some background scenery for your small worlds. Use card from cartons or boxes and paint mountains, cities, other planets, castles or other places to make the world more realistic. Take some photos of your creations for a story book or class collection, which you could use as an ideas book for stories and poems.

◆ Try to get a plastic aquarium and make an underground world with tunnels and caves that you can see though the sides.

# Materials, websites, books and other references

## Materials

Small world animals and people are available from all educational suppliers. There is a huge variety and range of types in suppliers catalogues and on their websites. Many suppliers have 'own brand' versions of small world sets, which are often cheaper, but may not be as realistic or durable. As with all educational equipment, you will get what you pay for - buy the best you can afford. For instance: ASCO **www.ascoeducational.co.uk** have Counting Kids (a box of 100 small world children), collections of insects, frogs etc, a collection of woodland animals.

Early Learning Centre **www.elc.co.uk** have baby wild animals, dinosaur models of various sizes and farm animals.

Britains **www.toyandmodel.com/britains** have a huge range of farm animals in families, farm vehicles, tractors and farm people. They also make fences, hay bales, animal shelters etc.

Playmobil **www.playmobil.com** have themed characters and a great range of fantasy settings, vehicles and accessories which are firm favourites of all children.

Consortium groups can often offer class or group Lego and other sets with huge numbers of pieces. Add some more specialised pieces, wheels, people, trees etc. from local suppliers or the Lego website **www.lego.com** for variety and inspiration.

## Books

Some more books for young readers who may need a bit of new inspiration:

**Where the Forest Meets the Sea**; Jeannie Baker; Walker Books

**The Sand Horse**; Ann Turnbull; Andersen Press

**Sand Sister**; Amanda White; Barefoot Books

**The Great Kapok Tree**; Lynne Cherry; Harcourt

**A Walk in the Rainforest**; Kristin Joy Pratt; Dawn Publications

**Amazon River Rescue**; Amanda Lumry; Eaglemont Press

**The Case of the Dinosaur in the Desert**; Pauline Hutchens-Wilson; Moody Publishers (A New Sugar Street Gang Story).

# Gardens

## Previous experience

Making gardens is a classic childhood activity, whether they are for superheroes or doll's tea parties. Children may have had experience of making gardens:

- in free play indoors and out of doors
- combined with small world to make story settings
- combined with fantasy worlds (dinosaurs, princes and princesses, wizards and dragons, superheroes etc)
- combined with malleable materials to make habitats for toys, creatures, vehicles
- to explore natural materials such as petals, leaves, seeds, stones, bark and twigs
- to explore free recall of stories they have heard and experiences they have had in real life
- to explore relationships and feelings in small world play.

## The responsive adult

In the early stages of working with these materials it is crucial to continue to observe the children. Only by doing this can you set developmentally appropriate challenges and provocations. The ideas listed here are offered as suggestions; the most exciting challenges will arise from children's own interests and motivations, which will only become apparent as you spend time with them, watching and joining them in their play. As you do this, you will be moving between the three interconnecting roles of observer, co-player, extender described below, and will be able to decide what you need to do next to take the learning forward. In three interconnecting roles, the responsive adult will be:

### Observer

- observing
- listening
- interpreting

### Co-player

- modelling
- playing alongside
- offering suggestions
- responding sensitively
- initiating with care!

### Extender

- discussing ideas
- sharing thinking
- modelling new skills
- asking open questions
- being an informed extender
- instigating ideas and thoughts
- supporting children as they make links in learning
- making possibilities evident
- introducing new ideas and resources
- offering challenges and provocations

## Offering challenges and provocations

Making gardens is a creative and therapeutic activity, which most children love. In the Foundation Stage this will probably have been a free choice, child-initiated activity, and you may have to sit with the children and help them to keep on task if you want to challenge their creativity in particular ways. Some children may never have made a miniature garden, so be patient and give plenty of scope for individual responses! Builders' trays are ideal, but paper or plastic plates are good for individuals.

- Can you make a garden with stones, pebbles and sand? Now go outside and collect some other things to make your garden more interesting. You can use anything you find, just make sure it will fit.

- Choose three small world animals or people and make a garden for them.

- Can you make a garden for some dinosaurs? They need plenty of things to eat.

- Find some foil and make a riverside or seaside garden, or a pond in a garden. Add some other objects and people to make it more realistic.

- Make a playground for children. Design it first on paper, then collect the things you need.

- Make a garden with just sand and leaves of different sorts, sizes and shapes. Use them to make paths and flower beds as well.

- Make a garden for a story character. Take some photos and make your own book to show with the story book.

- Look carefully at a real life garden (your own at home or one you like). Take some photos if you can. Now recreate your garden in the sand tray, making it as realistic as you can. Use anything that makes the garden look interesting, foil, small furniture, people, pets, animals and birds. You could draw these or cut them from gardening magazines or catalogues. Stick them on card and find a way to make them stand up.

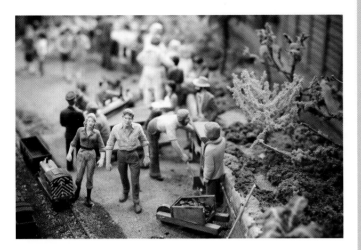

## Ready for more?

♦ What sort of garden would a superhero like? Design and make it for them. Add some character pictures that you have drawn or cut from magazines.

♦ Can you make a garden for a person who likes sitting and reading out of doors? You will need to think about the weather! Draw your ideas, then make a model of your garden.

♦ Design and make a garden with no plants. Think about what else can go in a garden to make it look interesting and welcoming.

♦ Get some grass seed and sprinkle it on damp sand or mud. Don't forget to water it with a small sprayer while it grows into a lawn.

♦ Collect some twigs, branches and leaves and make a garden for hedgehogs, frogs, toads and lizards. Make some animals from dough, clay or plasticene to live in your garden.

♦ Make a garden for your favourite story character (or a favourite member of your family). Fill it with the things they like.

♦ Try growing some real plants in sand. You could try hyacinth, daffodil or tulip bulbs or beans and peas. If you put the sand in a clear plastic bottle (the bottom of a water bottle works well) you will be able to see the roots growing. Remember to water them, but don't let them get too wet. Take a series of photos or drawings of the growth of your plants.

# Materials, websites, books and other references

## Materials

Making gardens is a therapeutic and creative activity. The children can quickly collect the natural materials they need from home or school, and you can add an occasional bargain bunch of flowers or some leaves or twigs you have collected.

You can use plates, old trays, plant saucers, shallow plastic boxes, packaging trays, or other shallow, waterproof containers as bases. This way, several children can work at the same time, and inspire each other. If they need some ideas, offer some gardening books or go on a local walk to look at gardens in the neighbourhood.

## Google images

* flower
* garden
* garden design
* flowerbed
* parterre

## Books

**How Does your Garden Grow?** Clare Matthews; Hamlyn Roots

**Shoots, Buckets and Boots**; Sharon Lovejoy; Workman Publishing

**Gardening with Children**; Kim Wilde; Harper Collins.

## Websites

Look at some websites of garden designers:

**www.gardenplans.com** has hundreds of garden plans to look at and download.

**www.applegategardens.co.uk** — look at 'garden design' for lots of lovely ideas for different sorts of gardens.

**www.bbc.co.uk/gardening/design** has lots of designs by TV garden designers.

**www.gardendesigner.com** where you can view and download free designs.

**www.rhs.org.uk/advice/design/design2** — for pictures of Chelsea.

**www.uktv.co.uk/index.cfm/uktv/Gardens** for children's garden plans.

**www.bbc.co.uk/gardening/gardening_with_children** — lots of ideas, projects, things to do.

**www.allotments-uk.com/links/gardening** for kids

**www.gardenorganic.org.uk/schools_organic_network/index** — a good site with ideas, curriculum links, activities etc, which might help with designing a garden.

**www.ltl.org.uk Learning Through Landscapes** is an inspiring charitable organisation which will help with information on all aspects of the outdoors. Look at some of the projects they have supported.

# Sand and moulding

## Previous experience

Moulding sand is a popular activity in the Foundation Stage. Delta Sand is a commercial version of sand, which is more permanent and can be sculpted. Children would have used sculpting and moulding techniques in sand:

- in free play with sand and mud indoors and out of doors

- combined with small world people and other figures to make habitats, roadways, bridges and tunnels

- with sand and malleable materials to make models and structures

- to explore shape, texture and form

- to count and order

- to explore pattern and repeating patterns.

## The responsive adult

In the early stages of working with these materials it is crucial to continue to observe the children. Only by doing this can you set developmentally appropriate challenges and provocations. The ideas listed here are offered as suggestions; the most exciting challenges will arise from children's own interests and motivations, which will only become apparent as you spend time with them, watching and joining them in their play. As you do this, you will be moving between the three interconnecting roles of observer, co-player, extender described below, and will be able to decide what you need to do next to take the learning forward. In three interconnecting roles, the responsive adult will be:

### Observer

- observing
- listening
- interpreting

### Co-player

- modelling
- playing alongside
- offering suggestions
- responding sensitively
- initiating with care!

### Extender

- discussing ideas
- sharing thinking
- modelling new skills
- asking open questions
- being an informed extender
- instigating ideas and thoughts
- supporting children as they make links in learning
- making possibilities evident
- introducing new ideas and resources
- offering challenges and provocations

## Offering challenges and provocations

Provide a range of moulds for sand and Delta Sand, including moulds made for sand and jelly. Collect small metal and plastic containers such as flower pots, yogurt pots, plastic caps of different sizes, little cups and bowls, shells, trays from chocolate boxes, cakes and tarts, plastic inserts from packaging and egg cartons.

- Explore all the different moulds and packaging and choose some favourites to make patterns and designs.

- Make a repeating pattern of two or three different sand moulds. See if your friend can continue the pattern.

- Use moulds with some coloured sand to make patterns and designs like chocolates and sweets. Decorate them with sequins or beads.

- Use some bigger moulds to make castles or blocks and decorate these with beads, sequins, shells and pebbles.

- Use a shallow flat tray to make a mould that you can write on with a sharp stick or a pencil. Now you can draw pictures, make patterns or write messages to your friends. A plant spray filled with water will keep the sand damp, so your marks don't disappear.

- Make some towers or other moulds with the sand and then make walls to link them into a castle or city wall.

- Look around at home and at school, for more ordinary and unusual objects that can be used as moulds with sand. Take some photos of the moulds and the patterns they make. You could make a catalogue for other children to use, with photos of the mould and what the sand looks like after moulding.

- Have a sandcastle competition with your friends. In pairs, take turns to make the best castle you can, take some photos of it and then let the next pair have a go. Ask your teacher to look at the castles and the photos and judge the winner.

## Ready for more?

♦ Look for jelly moulds in car boot sales and charity shops. Use these to make bigger models and castles, and decorate them with sequins, shells, stones, glass beads. You could also use these moulds to make castles of ice, cooked rice, clay or mud.

♦ Make a village or a whole city with small moulds. You could add white glue to the sand so the moulds don't dry out. Add gravel streets, people and vehicles to your city. Could you use the same method to make a fantasy scene with mountains, castles, bridges and houses?

♦ Get some Delta Sand and see what you can do with it. It's not as easy as it looks on the box! Take photos and make a book of tips for modelling with this 'sticky sand'.

♦ Look up 'sandcastle competition' on Google Images and see what you can find. Use the pictures as ideas for new ways of making sand look like stone. Have a new competition for making animals or landscapes with moulds and free work in the sand.

♦ Expand your collection of moulds and sand shapers by collecting foil dishes, cups, plastic bowls, shells, and other containers.

♦ Try making moulds with very wet sand and then freezing them overnight. What happens?

# Materials, websites, books and other references

## Materials

Use your ingenuity to find as many containers for moulding as you can. Packaging is a great source. Search for unusual sorts of sand moulds and jelly moulds to add — car boot sales, charity shops, bargain shops and cookware catalogues will often offer new ideas.

Add a range of small objects to decorate moulded sand — shells, sequins, beads, seeds, unusual items from pot pourri such as dried flowers and seed cases, buttons, badges, small world figures, cutlery etc.

Delta Sand, a mouldable sort of sand is available from **www.deltasand.com** where you can also see some finished projects. This sand is very different from plain sand and some children may become frustrated by it — give some time and support.

Another unusual sort of sand is Underwater Sculpting Sand which clings together for moulding underwater, but returns to its former state when you remove it from the water **www.amazon.co.uk** stock this product.

## Google Images

For images of sand sculptures try:

- sandcastle
- sand art
- sand sculpture
- sand figure
- beach sculpture
- beach art.

## Books

Some suitable books for younger children include:

**Art from Sand and Earth**; Gillian Chapman; Hodder Wayland

**Drawing in the Sand**: Jerry Butler; Zino Press Children's Books: a book about African American artists.

**Super Sand Castle Saturday (Mathstart)**; Stuart Murphy; Harper Collins

**Sandcastles Made Simple**; Lucinda Weirenga; Stewart, Tabori, Chang

**The Sand Horse**; Ann Turnbull; Andersen Press: a sand horse comes to life

**Sand** (Little Hands); Rachael Matthews; Chrysalis.

# Model buildings

## Previous experience

Children may have had experience of working with a variety of moulds and containers:

- making mud pies and sand castles

- packing sand into containers of different sizes and shapes, and tipping it out

- moulding wet sand with their hands

- exploring spatial relationships on 3D

- moving sand around to create hills, tunnels and smooth areas

- pushing and poking things into sand - brushes, sticks, pencils, flags

- making impressions in sand

- adding water to sand and exploring what happens.

## The responsive adult

In the early stages of working with these materials it is crucial to continue to observe the children. Only by doing this can you set developmentally appropriate challenges and provocations. The ideas listed here are offered as suggestions; the most exciting challenges will arise from children's own interests and motivations, which will only become apparent as you spend time with them, watching and joining them in their play. As you do this, you will be moving between the three interconnecting roles of observer, co-player, extender described below, and will be able to decide what you need to do next to take the learning forward. In three interconnecting roles, the responsive adult will be:

### Observer

- observing
- listening
- interpreting

### Co-player

- modelling
- playing alongside
- offering suggestions
- responding sensitively
- initiating with care!

### Extender

- discussing ideas
- sharing thinking
- modelling new skills
- asking open questions
- being an informed extender
- instigating ideas and thoughts
- supporting children as they make links in learning
- making possibilities evident
- introducing new ideas and resources
- offering challenges and provocations

## Offering challenges and provocations

Provide a range of small metal and plastic containers such as small flower pots, yogurt pots, plastic caps of different sizes, little cups and bowls, shells, little plastic bottles, plastic trays from chocolate boxes, cakes and tarts, egg cartons etc. You could also provide pictures of structures and buildings as inspiration for their constructions.

- Could you add strips of card or thin wood to extend your skills of building?

- Can you build a house, block of flats, church, railway station using sand and the pots and lids?

- Can you build a column of sand to support a small figure — like Nelson's Column?

- Can you make a home for a toy dinosaur or other jungle or wild animal?

- Can you build a tower with a series of moulds that decrease in size?

- Measure out a bowl or small bucket of sand. What is the highest structure you can build from this sand and the small moulding shapes? What is the longest structure you can make?

- Choose a small mould and see if you can build a structure using just this one mould. Can you make something from 20 mouldings? Or 30? Or 100? You may need to draw the design first.

- Can you make a replica of the Coliseum, the Great Wall of China, the Acropolis?

- Look in the recycled materials for some containers that you could use as moulds. You could cut some plastic containers to make different shapes and sizes, or cut card and stick it together to make little box shapes.

- Try cutting some plastic containers or water bottles. Look around the classroom for containers that you could use for moulding bricks and shapes from sand.

## Ready for more?

◆ Add tubes, boxes and card to your collection of moulds. Can you make a skyline or a whole city with these?

◆ Can you make a city of the future and add rockets and people?

◆ Collect lots of different moulds. Which ones work best? Why? Make a chart of what you discover.

◆ Make a plan or write a description for a structure or city. Challenge your friend to build it.

◆ Use the moulds to make some sleeping creatures — dinosaurs, dragons, monsters in the sand. They could be almost covered with the sand, like fossils or frozen in a deep freeze!

◆ Get some clay or mud and mix it with some sand. Use your moulds to make some bricks. Leave them to dry and then use them to make walls, buildings and other structures.

◆ Can you make a very, very small village with damp sand? Use cocktail sticks, small spoons, lolly sticks or twigs to help you with the details of doors, windows, gardens and fields. Find or make some tiny people and animals to live in your tiny village.

◆ Flatten out some damp sand and use a pencil or a stick to make mazes in the surface. Challenge a friend to find their way.

## Materials

Educational suppliers have endless supplies that can help with these activities. Look for small scoops, bun tins and cases, sand moulds and small objects to make patterns and impressions in the surface.

Recycled materials also offer lots of opportunities to work on a small scale. These include:

■ the liners from boxes of chocolates

■ small foil cases from cakes and pies

■ plastic caps of all sorts and sizes

■ aerosol caps

■ ice cream spoons, straws, ice cream cups

■ packaging plastic that you can cut down to make interesting shapes

■ coins, shells and buttons.

## Google images

• miniature

• miniature houses

• doll's house

• model great wall of China

• model acropolis

• model city

• wall

• tower

• Nelson's column

# Materials, websites, books and other references

## Websites

Try www.museumofminiatures.org for doll's houses.

www.essexminiatures.co.uk where you can click on individual models of Romans and Ancient Britons.

www.goodies-dollshouse-miniatures.co.uk has a new photo of a miniature every week.

## Books

Avoid Working on the Great Wall of China: Jacqueline Morley; Book House

The Great Wall; Elizabeth Mann; Miyaka Press

The Roman Colosseum; Elizabeth Mann; Miyaka Press

Skyscrapers and Bridges - Super Structures to design and build; Carol Johmann; Williamson

Structures, Materials and Art Activities; Barbara Taylor; Crabtree Publishing.

# Coloured sand

## Previous experience

Children will have had wide experience of pouring and sieving dry sand. They should have experimented with filling, emptying and moving sand in:

- free play with indoors and outside, with and without tools.

They may also have worked with other dry materials such as:

- soil
- grit
- peat
- compost
- bark
- gravel
- rice
- lentils
- glitter
- salt
- flour
- beans
- grass seed
- small beads.

## The responsive adult

In the early stages of working with these materials it is crucial to continue to observe the children. Only by doing this can you set developmentally appropriate challenges and provocations. The ideas listed here are offered as suggestions; the most exciting challenges will arise from children's own interests and motivations, which will only become apparent as you spend time with them, watching and joining them in their play. As you do this, you will be moving between the three interconnecting roles of observer, co-player, extender described below, and will be able to decide what you need to do next to take the learning forward. In three interconnecting roles, the responsive adult will be:

## Observer

- observing
- listening
- interpreting

## Co-player

- modelling
- playing alongside
- offering suggestions
- responding sensitively
- initiating with care!

## Extender

- discussing ideas
- sharing thinking
- modelling new skills
- asking open questions
- being an informed extender
- instigating ideas and thoughts
- supporting children as they make links in learning
- making possibilities evident
- introducing new ideas and resources
- offering challenges and provocations

## Offering challenges and provocations

Colouring sand may be a new experience in itself. Allow plenty of time for experimenting with colouring the sand, and free play before embarking on challenges.

- Fill a pouring bottle with sand. Can you write your name or a message with the sand?

- Can you make a permanent picture by using sticky-backed plastic? Fix the plastic down (sticky side up) using Blutack.

- Can you design and make a repeating sand pattern with different colours and shapes? You could use spoons, pouring bottles, shakers or just your hands to make the patterns. You could try drawing the design on paper and pouring the sand into the design.

- Can you make a template or stencil for making repeating patterns?

- Make more patterns with zigzags, circles, lines, crosses of different colours. Try pouring sand onto perspex or glass, so you can see right through the patterns you make.

- Find some other small objects to add to the sand or to your pictures. Glitter, rice, gravel and sequins all work well.

- Use coloured sand and other objects to make a portrait of a friend. Take a photo to preserve your picture.

- Use the coloured sand to make mountains, valleys and dunes. Add some animals or vehicles to your landscape.

- Find a small container with different colours of sand so it makes layers. How can you fill the layers of different coloured sand so they don't mix up? (look at Google 'sandlady' for some ideas).

- Find a straw. Can you make patterns by blowing gently at the sand with the straw? Be careful when you blow, so the sand doesn't get in your eyes. What is the best distance to blow from to make a controlled line?

## Ready for more?

- Explore pouring sand onto different sorts of papers, card and wallpaper. Try to get some embossed paper samples to try. How does the sand behave on different papers? Record what happens with a camera or on a chart.

- Devise some different containers for pouring sand. Try different shapes, sizes, numbers of holes. Use recycled containers, such as water bottles, cans or juice boxes.

- Can you find some different ways of making coloured sand? Which way is best? Make a sand recipe book for all the different kinds, so your friends can make them too.

- Can you make a maze or labyrinth by pouring sand, or by making paths through a tray of sand?

- Put the word 'aboriginal art' or 'mandala' in Google Images. Can you make some sand patterns and pictures like this?

- Experiment with adding other things to the sand. Try seeds, lentils, gravel, small beads etc. How can you make the sand flow more quickly? More slowly? How can you make it pile up higher?

- Use string and glue to make a pattern on wood or card, then pour sand over to make embossed patterns.

- Make glue patterns on card, then pour sand over before it dries. Tip off the extra sand to reveal your picture or pattern.

# Materials, websites, books and other references

## Materials

Coloured sand is available from lots of suppliers, just Google **coloured sand** to get hundreds of addresses. Here are a few:

Sand in lots of colours, bottles and gems to hide are available from **www.crazysand.co.uk**

Gravel, coloured sand and aggregates (not fine sand) from **www.rista.co.uk**

All sorts of sand bottles from **www.sandlady.co.uk**

For a good range of colours in shaker bottles at a reasonable price try **www.crafty-devils.com**

You could make your own coloured sands by using silver sand, colouring it with food colouring or paint and drying it in a warm oven or the sun. Don't dry it in a microwave, it will explode and do terminal damage to the microwave!!!

TTS Group sell food colouring in bargain sized bottles **www.tts-group.co.uk**

ASCO **www.ascoeducational.co.uk** have glitter in big bottles with shakers. Or use salt pots, plastic ketchup or mustard bottles, cooking oil containers or just plastic water bottles with a hole poked in the top for drizzling and pouring sand onto trays or paper.

Ask for wallpaper sample books or ends of rolls from decorators or DIY stores.

## Websites

Pictures of the Isle of Wight and Alum Bay **www.soton.ac.uk**

Pictures of erosion of sand cliffs **www.stacey.peak-media. co.uk/IoW/IsleofWight**

The site of a glass manufacture on the isle of Wight

**www.wightonline.co.uk/alumbayglass**

## Google Images

For images of coloured sand and cliffs, try:

- alum bay sands
- coloured sand
- sand art
- sand cliffs
- sand erosion
- sand cliff erosion
- glass makers

## Books

**Sand Art;** Top That Publishing (KIT and ideas)

**Art from Sand and Earth;** Gillian Chapman; Hodder Wayland

**Sand to Glass Welcome Books: How Things are Made;** Inez Snyder; Children's Press

**Sand Art;** Cheryl Owen; Walter Foster.

# Maps and landscapes

## Previous experience

Very young children need practice in being able to see two dimensional representations of landscapes. Making 3D maps and landscapes helps with this, and children may have been involved in:

- free play indoors and out of doors
- combining maps with miniatures - figures, buildings, vehicles
- using play mats of streets, cities, airports, harbours
- sharing stories where maps and plans appear
- drawing routes from home, plans of familiar places
- looking at maps, plans, atlases, diagrams
- looking for local features on walks and visits.

## The responsive adult

In the early stages of working with these materials it is crucial to continue to observe the children. Only by doing this can you set developmentally appropriate challenges and provocations. The ideas listed here are offered as suggestions; the most exciting challenges will arise from children's own interests and motivations, which will only become apparent as you spend time with them, watching and joining them in their play. As you do this, you will be moving between the three interconnecting roles of observer, co-player, extender described below, and will be able to decide what you need to do next to take the learning forward. In three interconnecting roles, the responsive adult will be:

### Observer

- observing
- listening
- interpreting

### Co-player

- modelling
- playing alongside
- offering suggestions
- responding sensitively
- initiating with care!

### Extender

- discussing ideas
- sharing thinking
- modelling new skills
- asking open questions
- being an informed extender
- instigating ideas and thoughts
- supporting children as they make links in learning
- making possibilities evident
- introducing new ideas and resources
- offering challenges and provocations

## Offering challenges and provocations

Encourage children to add objects and materials to sand for these activities. They may need some ideas from you to get them started. Encourage them to collect natural materials and bring things from home to add to their creations.

- Can you make a map of your way to school, using sand, stones, gravel and bricks?
- Can you make a map of the school, with your classroom, the hall, the playground and the garden or field?
- Use sand, stones, gravel, leaves and other objects to make a garden. It can be a real one or an imaginary one.
- Choose a story that you like. Now make a landscape for part of the story. You could make some characters as well as a scene or map.
- Could you use some foil, sand and crumpled paper to make a moon map?
- Can you make a map of a beach with sea, a pier, some boats and other seaside things?

- Use sand, stones, boxes, small bricks, plastic, fabric, leaves and twigs to make a dinosaur landscape with small world dinosaurs and prehistoric trees; or a jungle landscape with animals, plants and a river; or a medieval landscape with a castle, knights and horses, a moat and a forest.
- Make a treasure island in the sand. Find some twigs and leaves for trees, make a lake or pond, bury a treasure and draw a treasure map so your friends can hunt for the treasure.
- Can you make an island surrounded by water? Think about it before you start, so you don't flood the classroom!
- Can you make a replica of your own garden with sand, gravel and stones? Use a box to make your house.

## Ready for more?

♦ Work with some friends to make a bigger landscape or aerial views of real places. Try an airport, a building site, a space launch pad, a motorway, a safari park, a fairground or a farm. Use Google to find pictures and other information to help you.

♦ Try making bigger fantasy landscapes. You could design these together and then share the work of making them. How about a fantasy school, a park with new sorts of rides and equipment, a prehistoric theme park, an adventure land, a new planet or a castle just for kids?

♦ Look in Yellow Pages and ring or write to some local architects and builders. Ask them if they could come and talk about how they make plans and design new buildings and developments. They might let you have some real plans and maps to use.

♦ Find a map, a globe or an atlas and choose a country. Make a map of the country you choose. If you use a blue cloth for the sea it will be more realistic. Make the mountains, beaches and towns, using your own ideas for different parts and surfaces. You could work on your own or with friends.

♦ Find some model railway websites and request some catalogues for ideas for landscapes and models to make yourselves.

# Materials, websites, books and other references

## Materials

For miniature equipment such as buildings, people and other objects use Lego, Playmobil and other small world models already in your school or try:

www.asco.co.uk for a set of City Blocks - wooden models of houses and other buildings

www.toypost.co.uk for a Little Wooden Village and Little Wooden Farm

www.gltc.co.uk (Great Little Trading Company) for Garage Town, Pirate Island, Metropolis Train sets.

Shops, websites and catalogues for model train enthusiasts will provide people, animals, vehicles, trees, bushes, fences and other objects in a range of different scales for perfectionists!

## Websites

You will almost certainly have maps and atlases in school. Try to get some aerial photos of the area, or take photos of model layouts the children make. Make a map book of children's routes to school, the school plans, the way to get to local places. Some websites for aerial photos are:

www.earth.google.com — a site for seeing everywhere, but a bit difficult to use

www.multimap.com — click on aerial photos for some free examples to look at

www.ukaerialphotos.com — click on **Gallery** for some example images of theme parks, bridges, sports stadiums etc.

www.webbaviation.co.uk for county by county aerial photos

www.maps.google.co.uk will give you maps of anywhere by postcode, address, street name or locality. So will www.streetmap.co.uk, and www.ordnancesurvey.co.uk (maps of the UK)

www.wildgoose.ac have aerial photos, maps and a range of other geographical resources.

## Google Images

• model
• miniature
• train set.

• ariel view
• architectural models (this one has some very interesting images!)

## Books

There's a Map on My Lap! All about Maps; Tish Rabe; Random House

As the Crow Flies: A First Book of Maps; Gail Hartman; Athaeneum Books

Buried Blueprints; maps of lost worlds; Albert Lorenz; Harry Abrahams

Looking at Maps and Globes; Carmen Bredeson; Children's Press

Mapping Penny's World; Loreen Leedy; Henry Holt

Rosie's Walk; Pat Hutchens; Scholastic.

Wood; Andy Goldsworthy; Harry N. Abrams

# Diggers and excavators

## Previous experience

Most children, and particularly boys, will have had experience of using plastic or metal diggers, dump trucks, tipper lorries and other construction vehicles in sand, gravel and mud. They will probably have used them:

- in trays with sand, compost and mud
- in free play indoors and outside
- for scooping gravel or stones
- with small world people in construction play
- for solving spatial problems and building structures
- with logs, sticks and stones to make scenes and environments
- in role-play, while wearing construction worker hats and clothes.

## The responsive adult

In the early stages of working with these materials it is crucial to continue to observe the children. Only by doing this can you set developmentally appropriate challenges and provocations. The ideas listed here are offered as suggestions; the most exciting challenges will arise from children's own interests and motivations, which will only become apparent as you spend time with them, watching and joining them in their play. As you do this, you will be moving between the three interconnecting roles of observer, co-player, extender described below, and will be able to decide what you need to do next to take the learning forward. In three interconnecting roles, the responsive adult will be:

### Observer

- observing
- listening
- interpreting

### Co-player

- modelling
- playing alongside
- offering suggestions
- responding sensitively
- initiating with care!

### Extender

- discussing ideas
- sharing thinking
- modelling new skills
- asking open questions
- being an informed extender
- instigating ideas and thoughts
- supporting children as they make links in learning
- making possibilities evident
- introducing new ideas and resources
- offering challenges and provocations

## Offering challenges and provocations

- Find out how all the diggers work, talk about their best features and choose a favourite to work with as you scoop and move sand or gravel.

- Use the diggers to make tracks in the sand. Take some photos of the different tracks they make.

- Can you use your favourite digger to scoop all the sand into one big pile, without using your hands?

- Practise tipping loads of sand from the tipper lorries, using the mechanisms on the toy.

- Can you use the diggers and trucks to make an absolutely smooth road across the sand tray? How did you do it?

- Put 'digger' in Google Images and in Google web, and see what you find. E-mail some digger firms for some leaflets.

- Take the diggers outside and see how well they work with mud or compost. Which one works best? Record your findings with photos or a chart.

- Look out for construction sites when you are out with your family. Watch what diggers do and how they move. Look at what happens when they go backwards. Take some photos if you can and bring them to school for reference when you are working with the sand.

- Use sand and different gravels with diggers. Look at how they move and scoop. Which materials are easiest to work with?

- Add some branches and small logs to the sand and make some mounds and caves with the diggers.

- Pile the sand up and find the best way to make tunnels in the sand, just using toy diggers. Take photos of the best ones. Now look on the internet for the way tunnels are made in real life.

## Ready for more?

◆ Can you design a digger scoop and build it in junk materials — look at some sand scoops for ideas. Test your scoops with real sand and evaluate their strengths and weaknesses.

◆ Use photos or film of diggers and other construction vehicles to make a Power Point presentation, a book or a video of how they work, or a construction story.

◆ Look on educational suppliers sites and see if you can find out about working diggers that kids can ride on. Get some catalogues or other information.

◆ Contact a local construction firm and ask if they would bring a digger to school so you can look at it safely, take photos and ask questions.

◆ Look in your library or a public library for books and stories about construction machinery. Can you find out about the biggest digger in the world? Write up how you found your information, so other people can find out too.

◆ Look at **www.diggerland.com** where you can download photos of all sorts of diggers and print them off. You can also request a brochure. When you have some information, make a display with a sand tray and toy diggers in front, and your pictures, photos and other information behind them. Make signs and labels and introduce your display to your class.

## Materials

There are hundreds of different toy diggers in many different sizes. Try putting **toy digger** in Google Images to find a long, long list of different diggers from the small, accurate die cast models supplied by Corgi and other toy manufacturers.

See Caterpillar construction machines at **www.cat.com** and click through to the shop for die cast construction models.

The British geological Survey site **www.bgs.ac.uk** has geological maps and photos.

## Google Images

- quarry
- digger
- sand
- scoop
- sandpile
- dune
- sand cliff

Some inspiration may come by trying some of these in **www.wikipedia.org** to get reference material and pictures.

## Websites

**www.hyundai.be/news/products/big-float-prefers-hyundai** to look at diggers that float.

Look at **www.virtualquarry.co.uk** (this needs a media player to look at a quarry at work).

**www.diggerland.com** is an adventure park where children can ride and drive diggers.

## Books

**Mike Mulligan and His Steam Shovel;** Virginia Lee Burton; Frances Lincoln (a long time favourite story)

**Are you my Mother?;** P D Eastman; Harper Collins (a baby bird falls from the nest and is eventually returned to its mother by a digger)

**Dazzling Diggers;** Tody Mitton; Kingfisher Books

**Diggers and Cranes;** Caroline Young; Usborne

**Diggers and Cranes;** Jim Pipe; Franklin Watts

**Drawing Trucks and Diggers;** Caterpillar

**Wild About Trucks and Diggers;** Caroline Bingham; Ticktock media and of course there is Bob the Builder!

**What if We Were Builders?;** Featherstone; A & C Black

## DVDs

Big Machines 1 - Diggers And Dumpers

Let's Look At Diggers

Ready 2 Learn - Diggers And Dumpers.

# Drainpipes and guttering

## Previous experience

Drainpipes, guttering and other plumbing materials are readily available from DIY superstores and can be used to enhance many kinds of play and investigation. Children may already have had experience of these materials in the Foundation Stage:

- in free play indoors and outside

- in sand and water play

- combined with small world figures to make bridges and tunnels

- to balance and build, exploring abstract and imaginative constructions

- combined with malleable materials such as dough, gloop, foam, clay, mud

- to explore sliding, rolling, pouring and filling with toy cars, objects, abstract shapes, natural materials such as stones, seeds etc.

## The responsive adult

In the early stages of working with these materials it is crucial to continue to observe the children. Only by doing this can you set developmentally appropriate challenges and provocations. The ideas listed here are offered as suggestions; the most exciting challenges will arise from children's own interests and motivations, which will only become apparent as you spend time with them, watching and joining them in their play. As you do this, you will be moving between the three interconnecting roles of observer, co-player, extender described below, and will be able to decide what you need to do next to take the learning forward. In three interconnecting roles, the responsive adult will be:

### Observer

- observing
- listening
- interpreting

### Co-player

- modelling
- playing alongside
- offering suggestions
- responding sensitively
- initiating with care!

### Extender

- discussing ideas
- sharing thinking
- modelling new skills
- asking open questions
- being an informed extender
- instigating ideas and thoughts
- supporting children as they make links in learning
- making possibilities evident
- introducing new ideas and resources
- offering challenges and provocations

## Offering challenges and provocations

- Can you join (X) number of pieces of pipe together to make an interesting shape to pour sand through?

- What is the longest sand run of pipes and guttering you can make? Can you get sand to move all the way along it?

- How can you get sand to flow round corners?

- How many different ways can you find to join 4/5/6 pieces of pipe or guttering together?

- Can you make a marble run with sand, pipes, tape and guttering?

- Can you find a way to make sand run through a pipe without tilting it?

- Try using lentils, grass seed, bird food or dried peas instead of sand. Do these move through the pipes more easily? Which one is best? Take some photos of your experiments.

- Can you cut and join a series of empty plastic bottles together to make your own drainpipe?

- Go for a walk round your school and make drawings of the different ways that pipes, guttering and plumbing pipes are used. Look for the different joins between pipes. Look under sinks, outside, under the edges of the roof, and near radiators.

- On a rainy day, watch the gutters and rainpipes round your school. Does anything else apart from water come out? How could you catch some of the things that get washed down?

- Find or make some small pipes or pieces of tubing. Can you use these to fill toy trucks with sand and gravel? How can you steady the little pipes so the sand goes into the truck when you are using your hands to pour with?

## Ready for more?

- Try joining pipes together with different materials — duct tape, fabric, sellotape, sticky tac. Which works best? Record what you find out, using a camera, clipboard, database or chart.

- Collect or make some pipes and tubes of different diameters and materials. Test them to find which ones work best for moving sand.

- Add some figures or animals to the sand and see if you can move them through your constructions.

- Can you find a way to support the guttering and pipes so the sand can flow downhill.

- Can you build a sand cascade?

- Can you fix 2 or 3 pipes together in a bunch so you can fill containers more quickly?

- Put 'Pompidou' in Google images for pictures of plumbing on the outside of buildings.

- Can you make a sand 'shower head' like a water shower?

- Make the longest length of pipe you can by fixing drainpipes together. It may be easier to do this outside. Now explore different ways of making the pipe slope by propping the end up. Send sand, gravel, stones or beads down the long pipe. Which angle is best for making sure all the sand comes out at the end? Which angle makes the sand run fastest?

# Materials, websites, books and other references

## Materials

The best value in guttering and drainpipes will be found locally at builders' merchants and DIY superstores. Get straight bits and some joints and bends. Flexible joints make good additions. Add some duct tape (the silver stuff), and try to get this at bargain or 'Pound' shops where it will be much cheaper.

If you can afford to buy something from an educational supplier, try the wooden viaduct from Asco **www.ascoeducational.co.uk** or TTS **www.tts-group.co.uk** who stock a bamboo water channelling kit which could be used for sand too. Many suppliers have sand wheels and marble runs of different sorts that can be added to guttering and pipes for more challenges. Add some tubing (available from DIY shops and builders' merchants). This works with sand too!

Local plumbers may respond to a letter from the children, and donate some of these resources, or there may be a parent of children in the school who has links with the building trade.

Marble runs are good for sand too. You can get them from most educational suppliers, or toyshops, or make your own from cardboard tubes and guttering. The children may have to experiment with the slope of the runs to make the sand or gravel move, and you may want to add some small objects such as beads or pea gravel to sand to help the flow. **www.rista.co.uk** sell Diamonique beads in a range of colours, which might provide an alternative to sand.

## Google Images

Try

- Pompidou Centre
- Lloyd's building

to find pictures of two buildings with their plumbing on the outside. You could also try

- pipes
- burst water main
- guttering
- tubing
- plumbing
- fireman hose
- water pipes
- garden hose

## Books

A Day With a Plumber; Mark Thomas; Children's Press.

# Marks and patterns

## Previous experience

In the Foundation Stage, children will have had experience of mark making and patterning in a wide range of contexts and with different sorts of tools during both child initiated and adult directed learning. Children may have already had experience of:

- mark making in sand, mud, dough etc with hands, fingers, feet, and with tools like rakes, spades, forks

- painting drawing and printing

- patterning with pegboards and construction toys, shapes, bead threading etc

- making rubbings of patterned and textured surfaces

- working with 2D and 3D shapes

- free access to a mark making area with a range of materials and tools.

## The responsive adult

In the early stages of working with these materials it is crucial to continue to observe the children. Only by doing this can you set developmentally appropriate challenges and provocations. The ideas listed here are offered as suggestions; the most exciting challenges will arise from children's own interests and motivations, which will only become apparent as you spend time with them, watching and joining them in their play. As you do this, you will be moving between the three interconnecting roles of observer, co-player, extender described below, and will be able to decide what you need to do next to take the learning forward. In three interconnecting roles, the responsive adult will be:

### Observer

- observing
- listening
- interpreting

### Co-player

- modelling
- playing alongside
- offering suggestions
- responding sensitively
- initiating with care!

### Extender

- discussing ideas
- sharing thinking
- modelling new skills
- asking open questions
- being an informed extender
- instigating ideas and thoughts
- supporting children as they make links in learning
- making possibilities evident
- introducing new ideas and resources
- offering challenges and provocations

## Offering challenges and provocations

- Use combs of different sizes and shapes to make patterns in dry and damp sand.

- Collect some natural or man-made objects and make some patterns in dry or damp sand. Try nuts, seeds, stones, plastic caps, sticks, shells, counters, coins and glass beads.

- Can you make your own combs from card, plastic or polystyrene for making patterns? Which material works best? Which is easiest to cut?

- Make some coloured sand for pouring and combing into patterns? Can you use more than one colour?

- Find some toy cars and trucks, and use them to make patterns in the sand.

- Use a collection of objects to make a pattern of marks in damp sand. Can your friend match the objects with the marks you have made?

- Write a rhyme, song or poem in the sand, using a salt pot or other pourer.

- Write a message in the sand and leave it where other people can read it. See if you get any replies!

- Copy a pattern or a picture with only one finger. Try with the other hand — is it harder? Now try writing with both hands together.

- Hide something in shallow sand and make tracks or footprints as clues for your friend to find what you have hidden.

- Paint a piece of card with a mixture of white glue and water. Now sprinkle sand or draw patterns with a sand pourer on the glue before it dries. What happens to your sand pattern when it is dry?

- Explore how you could use a sieve or colander to make sand patterns. What did you find out? Try using different sorts of containers with holes.

## Ready for more?

♦ Bury wet paper or fabric in sand to make embossed patterns in damp sand.

♦ Use buttons, sequins, beads, Lego and other small objects to make patterns in dry or damp sand. Find the best way to get them out again when you have finished!

♦ Get everyone to write their name in wet sand, take some photos and make them into a calendar or a poster, or cards or gift tags.

♦ Make a word bank in the sand of all the words you can write. Take photos and make a display.

♦ Who can make the longest continuous line in the sand?

♦ Put some words in Google images (eg 'pattern', 'zigzag','stripes' 'animal print') and see if you can find some patterns to copy.

♦ Find a mark making tool and see how many marks you can make in a tray of sand — can you make 100? 200? 1000?

♦ Use empty plastic bottles and some string to find out how to make patterns with sand. Make holes in plastic bottles and suspend them over a tray or black paper, so the sand can come out of the holes you have made. Try different numbers of holes, and watch to see if the pattern changes when you swing the bottle gently on the string.

## Materials, websites, books and other references

### Materials

www.asco.co.uk for sand combs and rollers or TTS Group.

You can also use expired credit and store cards to make cheap combs for patterning. Just cut the edges with scissors to make different patterns. Or use stiff card or the plastic from milk and water bottles.

Pet combs and hair combs of all sorts will provide a source of different patterns (try Bargain and Pound shops for cheap versions).

Encourage children to collect sticks, twigs, old pencils, old toothbrushes and household tools for patterning.

Provide shallow trays (eg plant saucers, windowsill trays, builders' trays) of dry sand, which only need a finger to make patterns, pictures and letters!

### Google Images

• patterns sand          • sand sculpture

• sand ripples           • fossil footprints.

• footprints

### Websites

www.creativekidsathome.com have free-to-download Mandala templates and photos of the activity.

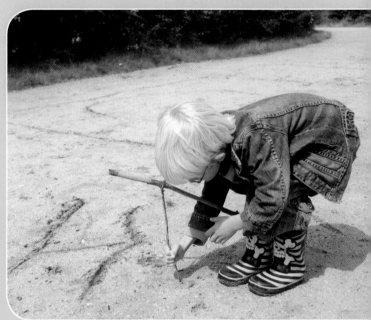

### Books

**Nature's Playground**; Fiona Danks; Frances Lincoln

**Pattern and Texture; and Colour**; Paul Flux; Heinemann

**Fun with Pattern and Shape**; Jenny Ackland; Oxford University Press

**Pattern**; Henry Pluckrose; Franklin Watts

**Patterns Everywhere**; Julie Dalton; Children;s Press

**Discover Science**; Pattern; Kim Taylor; Chrysalis

**Art from Sand and Earth**; Gillian Chapman; Hodder Wayland

**Mandala Colouring books**; (you could use these as patterns for sand art); Monique Mandali;

**Mandali Publishing** (available through Amazon)

**Sand Paintings of the Navaho**; Franc Johnson Newcomb; Dover Publications

# Hide and find

## Previous experience

Hiding and treasure hunts are fascinating for children of all ages. In the Foundation Stage many children will have experienced adult and child devised hide-and-find games in:

- free play indoors and in the garden
- in sand and other malleable materials
- in more formal games such as Hunt the Thimble, Hunt the Teddy, Find the Object
- in discussions relating to positional language (under, behind, in front, beside etc)
- making their own games of 'hide-and-find' or 'hide and seek' in their setting or at home
- reading and talking about hidden treasure in stories, rhymes, films, TV stories and fact books.

## The responsive adult

In the early stages of working with these materials it is crucial to continue to observe the children. Only by doing this can you set developmentally appropriate challenges and provocations. The ideas listed here are offered as suggestions; the most exciting challenges will arise from children's own interests and motivations, which will only become apparent as you spend time with them, watching and joining them in their play. As you do this, you will be moving between the three interconnecting roles of observer, co-player, extender described below, and will be able to decide what you need to do next to take the learning forward. In three interconnecting roles, the responsive adult will be:

### Observer

- observing
- listening
- interpreting

### Co-player

- modelling
- playing alongside
- offering suggestions
- responding sensitively
- initiating with care!

### Extender

- discussing ideas
- sharing thinking
- modelling new skills
- asking open questions
- being an informed extender
- instigating ideas and thoughts
- supporting children as they make links in learning
- making possibilities evident
- introducing new ideas and resources
- offering challenges and provocations

## Offering challenges and provocations

- Make a list of some small objects. Now hide them in a box or bowl of sand for your friend to find and check off on the list.

- Hide lots of small objects in a big box of sand. Set some challenges to find specific things or numbers of things — 5 dinosaurs, 6 buttons, 8 keys, 3 crabs, 10 coins etc.

- Put lots of dried peas, marbles or grains of rice in a sand box. How many can you find? Can you work out a good way of counting these very small things?

- Bury some objects and write descriptions of them instead of a list of their names — a green animal, a silver metal object etc. Challenge your friends to find them.

- Bury lots of objects, then make a graph of all the things you find.

- Bury lots of plastic letters. Now find the letters of your name, other words, or all the letters of the alphabet.

- Bury plastic numbers, then challenge your friend to find the answer to simple calculations — e.g. 'Can you find the answer to $3 + 5$?'

- Put 'buried treasure' in Google web and try some of the activities you find there.

- If you put sequins or small beads in sand, how can you get them out again? Experiment with different tools and methods. Draw pictures of your findings.

- Find six small objects. Draw each one on paper or card. Hide the objects and shuffle the pictures. Lay the pictures in a sequence and see if you can find the objects in the right order. Now challenge some friends.

- Make a mixture of dry sand, sequins, lentils, beans, beads and seeds. Use a timer or the clock to time how long it takes to sort all the things out again.

## Ready for more?

◆ Make a secret message in plastic letters. Bury your message and mix up the letters. Now challenge a friend to find the message.

◆ Make a treasure map and bury objects at special places shown on the map.

◆ Bury the pieces of a jigsaw in *dry* sand. Can you make the jigsaw by finding all the hidden pieces?

◆ Bury some old objects. Can you put them on a time line in chronological order when you have found them all?

◆ Find and hide some objects, then make up a story using each object as you find it. Put the objects in a row so you can remember your story. Now bury them again and make up a new story.

◆ Choose a pebble each. Look carefully at your own pebble and draw it. Bury all the pebbles and see if you can match them up with the drawings as you find each one.

◆ A game for two to four people. Find a scarf or blindfold (a soft fabric head band works well). Now bury some objects in the sand and take turns to wear the blindfold as you find an object and name it just by touch. If you are right, keep the object, if not, bury it again. The player with the most objects at the end of the game is the winner.

# Materials, websites, books and other references

## Materials

You can bury anything, here are some ideas:

■ foreign and out of circulation coins or plastic medals

■ bags of polished stones and pebbles, and glass beads are available in many bargain shops at bargain prices

■ shells and stones of unusual shapes

■ make a Christmas collection of the objects from crackers

■ many bargain shops have cheap bags of small animals, insects, dinosaurs etc

■ get beads and other jewels from charity shops and markets

■ jigsaws (preferably wooden ones that don't get damp in the sand)

■ sequins are cheap and come in all sorts of shapes and sizes

## Websites

www.philipandtacey.co.uk have a dazzling collection of sequins, beads, glass beads and other objects to hide in or mix with sand. You could even buy some of their bags of googly eyes to bury and find! They also have plastic letters and numbers.

www.outlandstone.co.uk sell stones and pebbles in lovely colours, look at the pictures, but you have to buy at least 25kg of each or share a bag!

www.emporiumuk.biz have a massive range of glass beads, marbles and other decorative beads.

## Google images

Suggestions for words to search:

• treasure
• treasure island
• treasure map
• pirate
• pirate ship
• gold
• jewels
• necklace
• beads.

## Books

**Treasure Island (Junior Classics)**; Robert Louis Stevenson; Naxos Audio Books (CD)

**Pirate Pete**; Kim Kennedy; Harry N Abrahams

**Noelle's Treasure Tale** - book and CD; Gloria Estefan; Rayo

**Pam's Maps**; Pippe Goodhart; Red Fox

**Felix and the Blue Dragon**; Angela McAllister; Orion Children's

**Berenstain Bears Seashore Treasure**; Stan Berenstain; Harper Collins

**Dolphin Treasure**; Wayne Grover; Harper Trophy

**Duncan Cameron's Shipwreck Detective**; Richard Platt; DK Publishing

# Imagined worlds

## Previous experience

Making environments for small world and other fantasy situations will be familiar to children. In the Foundation Stage they may have had experience of these materials:

- in free play indoors and out of doors
- combined with small world people and animals, vehicles etc
- combined with malleable materials such as clay or dough
- for story telling
- for exploring sequence, character and plot
- in sand, water, malleable materials, clay, gravel, compost, mud.

## The responsive adult

In the early stages of working with these materials it is crucial to continue to observe the children. Only by doing this can you set developmentally appropriate challenges and provocations. The ideas listed here are offered as suggestions; the most exciting challenges will arise from children's own interests and motivations, which will only become apparent as you spend time with them, watching and joining them in their play. As you do this, you will be moving between the three interconnecting roles of observer, co-player, extender described below, and will be able to decide what you need to do next to take the learning forward. In three interconnecting roles, the responsive adult will be:

### Observer
- observing
- listening
- interpreting

### Co-player
- modelling
- playing alongside
- offering suggestions
- responding sensitively
- initiating with care!

### Extender
- discussing ideas
- sharing thinking
- modelling new skills
- asking open questions
- being an informed extender
- instigating ideas and thoughts
- supporting children as they make links in learning
- making possibilities evident
- introducing new ideas and resources
- offering challenges and provocations

## Offering challenges and provocations

Children will probably have had free experience of these activities and materials, and may not be used to adult initiation or direction through specific challenges. You may have to go slowly and be patient if their focus strays and they play something completely different!

- Can you make a world for these dinosaurs/animals/knights/penguins/underwater creatures etc?
- Collect some twigs, leaves and other natural materials from home or the school garden and make an imagined forest or mountain side.
- Put some plastic animals and reptiles in a bag. Now take just one handful of creatures and make an environment for them.
- Put some word cards in the bag - 'jungle' 'desert' 'space' 'mountain' 'seaside'. Pull out one card and make the world it says.
- Using a flat builders' tray and some foil, make a space landscape. Add some spacemen or space monsters made from clay or plasticene.

- Draw a fantasy landscape for superheroes. Using the sand as a base, build some structures such as buildings, bridges and tunnels for the superheroes to move in. Now make up a superhero story with your friends, using the landscape.
- Make a sand tray world for your favourite story character. Add creatures, trees and plants, buildings or people. Take some photos of your landscape and make a new story book with your photos.
- Use sand and water to make a fantasy island. Add other objects and things you find to make your island as exciting and interesting as possible. Now use some animals or people to make up an island story. Tell your story to someone else when you have decided what it is.

## Ready for more?

◆ Work with some friends to design and make a fantasy landscape. Decide who will do the drawing, the research, the building, take the photos, do a commentary. Make sure you take photos right from the start of your project, and keep taking them throughout and at the end. Make a PowerPoint presentation of your project.

◆ Look on Google for some pictures of film and TV characters. Print off some pictures and stick them on card to make characters. Now make a scene for your character to inhabit.

◆ Be a film designer. Watch 'Finding Nemo', 'Jungle Book', 'Star Wars', 'Planet Earth' or another video and make some sets for the characters in the film. Draw the characters and stick on card or make them from plasticene. Or you could use the small toy versions of the film characters.

◆ Pick a story book and look carefully at one of the pictures. Can you make a replica with sand and other objects? Try to make the model as accurate as possible.

◆ How can you make a model volcano with the sand? Look for some pictures on Google images and have a go. What could you use to make molten lava flows and fire at the top of your volcano? Can you make the sand flow down the sides of your volcano? Make up an adventure story about this dangerous place.

## Materials

You will have many objects and materials for starting imagined world play in trays or small boxes of sand. These include:

■ dinosaurs and farm/zoo animals

■ fantasy characters, including the small versions of superhero toys

■ Playmobil, Lego and other characters from construction sets

■ comics, catalogues and magazines with pictures for the children to cut out and mount on card

■ clay, dough and plasticene for characters and models

■ add sawn logs, collect twigs and leaves, dig up some stones and pebbles

Film and TV characters are often good story starters for imagined world, ask the children to bring in favourites. And of course, any story you tell can be the start of a new activity for the children, making or finding their own character figures and making their own environments.

Look at **www.philipandtacey.co.uk** for Active World Mats — which are Builders' trays with sets of characters for small world imaginative play. TTS group **www.tts-group.co.uk** also stock these.

## Websites

You could also try some of the sites for teachers (in the UK and abroad) for activities and templates for making characters - here are a few:

**www.activitiesforkids.com** and **www.thekidzpage.com** have free clip art

**www.bbc.co.uk** has sections for schools and parents with activities and printable sheets.

# Materials, websites, books and other references

## Google images

• Disney

or enter the name of a character such as

| | |
|---|---|
| • Bambi | • Cinderella |
| • Nemo | • Lion King |
| • Superman | • volcano etc. |
| • princess | |

and Google web search for

| | |
|---|---|
| • Disney | • family.go.com |

or animal or character names.

## Books

There are so many suitable stories that we are not suggesting titles, but you could explore books on fantasy landscapes for older children, or titles on architectural models or theatre design.

# Caves and tunnels

## Previous experience

During their time in the Foundation Stage children will have experimented with making tunnels and caves in various ways during:

- free play indoors and outside, in sand and mud
- in wet sand
- by exploring the holes made by insects and small animals

They will have made caves and tunnels when:

- making dens with boxes and drapes
- playing with construction, small world toys and train tracks
- playing on large apparatus.

They may also have experienced being in tunnels in cars and trains, and some may have been through the Channel Tunnel or visited caves.

## The responsive adult

In the early stages of working with these materials it is crucial to continue to observe the children. Only by doing this can you set developmentally appropriate challenges and provocations. The ideas listed here are offered as suggestions; the most exciting challenges will arise from children's own interests and motivations, which will only become apparent as you spend time with them, watching and joining them in their play. As you do this, you will be moving between the three interconnecting roles of observer, co-player, extender described below, and will be able to decide what you need to do next to take the learning forward. In three interconnecting roles, the responsive adult will be:

### Observer

- observing
- listening
- interpreting

### Co-player

- modelling
- playing alongside
- offering suggestions
- responding sensitively
- initiating with care!

### Extender

- discussing ideas
- sharing thinking
- modelling new skills
- asking open questions
- being an informed extender
- instigating ideas and thoughts
- supporting children as they make links in learning
- making possibilities evident
- introducing new ideas and resources
- offering challenges and provocations

## Offering challenges and provocations

- Can you make a tunnel in the sand that a toy car can travel through?
- Can you make a tunnel that is strong enough for a toy car to go over the top?
- Who can make the widest, or the longest tunnel?
- Can you make a tunnel that turns a corner or goes round an obstacle?
- Can you work with a partner to make a tunnel, starting at opposite ends and meeting in the middle? Put 'Channel Tunnel' in Google to find out how they did it!
- Make a tunnel that Action man or Barbie can get through.
- Make a cave for a family of dinosaurs.
- Make a cave for a soft toy or a some small world animals that live in caves.

- Can you make a cave for some cave men? It needs a good lookout place, and to be safe from dangerous animals.
- Look in the library for some books about caves and tunnels. Take some photos of your caves and tunnels and make a display in your classroom.
- Some tunnels need strengthening or they collapse. How could you make your tunnels stronger?
- Make up a story about getting trapped in a tunnel, and tell the story by making the tunnel and using small world characters.
- Find a train track set (you may have to borrow one from another class). Now set the train track up in the sand tray and experiment with making tunnels for the trains to go through. You may need to use supports for your tunnels to make them longer and stronger.

## Ready for more?

- ◆ Draw a plan for a series of tunnels that connect with each other. Make the tunnels to match your plan. What are the difficulties with making tunnels? How can you overcome these?

- ◆ Make a building from Lego or boxes. Now put it in the sand and make a secret cave underneath the building. How can you support the building?

- ◆ Explore different ways of supporting and reinforcing tunnels and caves. What works best? Take some photos of your ideas.

- ◆ Plan and make a series of caves linked by tunnels. Add some play people and make up some adventure stories. If you take photos, you could make a story book for your friends to read.

- ◆ How can you use mirrors to look inside your tunnels and caves? Can you take a photo of the inside of a cave or tunnel? Can you make features on the roofs of the caves and tunnels?

- ◆ Find some pictures of cave animals. Try this site **www.kathimitchell.com** and click on 'caves' for some great ideas for making cave habitats. Look in your library for cave dwelling animals to live in the caves you have made.

- ◆ Use some thin fabric to dress some small world people as cave people and make a habitat for them with a cave, lookout and hunting area with animals.

## Materials

Collect materials for supporting and propping the sand — these could include:

- ■ fallen sticks, collected on walks to the woods
- ■ masking tape and duct tape from bargain and 'Pound' shops
- ■ offcuts of plywood or pieces of driftwood
- ■ card and plastic tubing, plastic bottles with the tops and bottoms cut off, plastic bowls and boxes
- ■ plastic netting, plaster bandage (such as Modroc).

## Google Images

- • cave
- • caving
- • tunnel
- • forest den
- • burrow
- • stalactite.

## Websites

The very best site about caves for teachers and children is **www.kathimitchell.com** click on 'caves' in the science section on the right of the page — it has lots of links to other sites about caves, cave animals, make your own stalactites, cave terms, photos, screen savers etc — you could spend a whole term here, using the links and information.

Other sites include:

**http.arachnophiliac.co.uk** — for spiders, snakes and other animals that live underground.

**www.wookey.co.uk** the site for Wookey Hole Caves, with photos.

**www.cheddarcaves.co.uk** and **www.whitescarcave.co.uk** which has a good virtual tour of the caves.

**www.caving.uk.com** is a site for cavers.

## Books

**I wonder why Stalactites Hang Down**; Jackie Gaff; Kingfisher

**I wonder why Tunnels are Round**; Steve Parker; Kingfisher

**Crypts, Caves and Tunnels of London**; Ian Marchant; Watling Street Ltd

**Cave animals (animals and their habitats)**; Francine Galko; Heinemann

**Caves**; Jeanne Hanson; Chelsea House

**The Dak-Dak series - the hidden caves of Oslama**; Susan Van de Leucht; Lulu.com

**The Channel Tunnel**; S Donvan; Lerner Publishing

# Story book creations

## Previous experience

Children will probably have had experience of working with story book characters in sand, especially those from traditional stories such as *The Gingerbread Man, Little Red Riding Hood* etc. These may have been in:

- free play both indoors and outside
- dressing up as story book characters
- using puppets to represent story characters
- using small world figures to develop story scenes or a narrative
- a wide range of traditional stories and picture books by significant authors
- working with wet and dry sand and gravel to explore its properties;
- using sand to create a range of habitats.

## The responsive adult

In the early stages of working with these materials it is crucial to continue to observe the children. Only by doing this can you set developmentally appropriate challenges and provocations. The ideas listed here are offered as suggestions; the most exciting challenges will arise from children's own interests and motivations, which will only become apparent as you spend time with them, watching and joining them in their play. As you do this, you will be moving between the three interconnecting roles of observer, co-player, extender described below, and will be able to decide what you need to do next to take the learning forward. In three interconnecting roles, the responsive adult will be:

### Observer

- observing
- listening
- interpreting

### Co-player

- modelling
- playing alongside
- offering suggestions
- responding sensitively
- initiating with care!

### Extender

- discussing ideas
- sharing thinking
- modelling new skills
- asking open questions
- being an informed extender
- instigating ideas and thoughts
- supporting children as they make links in learning
- making possibilities evident
- introducing new ideas and resources
- offering challenges and provocations

## Offering challenges and provocations

- Can you make a scene in the sand that could be used for the cover of a book you know?
- Can you make a scene that could be used as an advert or poster for one of your favourite books?
- Could you produce a series of scenes that would tell a story? This could either be one you already know or one you make up.
- Make an alternative ending to a story you know.
- Could you make a setting and use story book characters to help you tell a story to other children?
- Use plasticene, clay or dough to make some characters of your own. Use a digital camera to make a story with your characters.
- Collect some card, wood, twigs, string, stones, branches, foil, pebbles, shells and other objects to add to the sand to make your scenes and stories more interesting, exciting and varied.
- Use damp sand to make caves, towers, castles or cottages for your characters and stories. Find ways to support your structures, and spray them with water to keep the sand damp.
- Choose a story book and look closely at the pictures. Make a replica of one of the pictures using sand, gravel, pebbles, and other natural objects to help to make it realistic. Take some photos and make a display with your scene, characters and the story book.
- Get some branches and use them to make a cave for a story. Use some story characters to make up an exciting cave story. You could use fabric and card to turn Lego or Playmobil people into characters — a horse into a unicorn, a man into a king, a woman into a witch!

## Ready for more?

♦ Use a big sand tray to make a story map — e.g. Red Riding Hood's house, the woods, the path to Grandmother's house etc, or *Rosie's Walk* or *The Bear Hunt*.

♦ Can you produce and photograph 12 different story settings for a calendar?

♦ Could you produce a 'Guess the Story' book by producing a range of scenes and taking photos.

♦ Make a new story from an old one - e.g. *We're Going on a Dinosaur Hunt; The Three Tigers; Super Rabbit; The Magic Stone.*

♦ Make a story plan or a story board on paper, then make the scenes and characters for your own original story.

♦ Make settings for Doctor Who, films, Superman, favourite pop groups.

♦ Work as a class to make all the different scenes for a longer story such as *The Iron Man* or *The Hobbit*. You can make clothes for characters from thin fabric, and props from card or plastic. Make some backgrounds for your story by drawing or painting the scenes on pieces of card and bending or scoring them so they can stand up at the back of the sand tray. Add stones for rocks, boxes for buildings, twigs for trees and piles of sand for mountains. Take photos as you tell the story, so you can make a display.

## Materials

Recycled materials are free, so make sure the children have plenty of choice and can get the things they want to use as they work with sand and gravel.

Put a notice up inviting offers of *clean* recycled materials such as:

■ small cardboard tubes and boxes and cones, egg boxes

■ plastic bottles and tops, containers, cups, tubs and pots

■ plastic and polystyrene trays, bubble wrap

■ offcuts of paper and wallpaper, newspapers, junk mail and magazines

■ plastic and paper carriers, paper bags

■ string, wool, pipe cleaners, soft wire, cord and rope; sticks, twigs, small logs

■ scraps of fabric to make clothes for home made characters

Leave a box by the notice, so parents and children can drop their offerings in. Then you can sort and check them for suitability, Health and Safety and cleanliness.

It's important to give children plenty of time to work on their projects and to find some way of protecting unfinished projects, particularly if you are expecting them to photograph the story for a book or presentation.

TTS group **www.tts-group.co.uk** and Early Learning Centre have tough digital and video cameras that are easy for children to use.

## Google Images

To look at some recycled art and sculpture, try

• forest
• island
• farm
• tower.
• castle

# Materials, websites, books and other references

## Websites

Traditional story characters, scenes and other story telling resources from Yellow Door **www.yellow-door.net**

## Books

Collect a good range of picture books with illustrations that can inspire children's work. Discuss the story and the pictures as you encourage children to experiment with making scenes and enacting the stories. Encourage them to bring or make characters to inhabit the story landscapes they make.

| Literacy 1 Speaking | • Retell stories, ordering events using story language<br>• Tell stories and describe incidents from their own experience in an audible voice.<br>• Interpret a text by reading aloud with some variety in pace and emphasis<br>• Experiment with and build new stores of words to communicate in different contexts. | Literacy 6 Word structure and spelling | • Spell new words using phonics as the prime approach<br>• Segment sounds into their constituent phonemes in order to spell them correctly. Children move from spelling simple CVC words to longer words that include common diagraphs & adjacent consonants such as 'brush', 'crunch'<br>• Recognise and use alternative ways of spelling the graphemes already taught, for example that the /ae/ sound can be spelt with 'ai', 'ay' or 'a-e'; that the /ee/ sound can also be spelt as 'ea' and 'e'; & begin to know which words contain which spelling alternatives<br>• Use knowledge of common inflections in spelling, such as plurals, -ly, -er<br>• Read and spell phonically decodable two and three syllable words. | Literacy 8 Engaging and responding to text | • Select books for personal reading and give reasons for choices<br>• Visualise and comment on events, characters and ideas, making imaginative links to their own experiences<br>• Distinguish fiction and nonfiction texts and the different purposes for reading them. |
| Literacy 2 Listening and responding | • Listen with sustained concentration, building new stores of words in different contexts<br>• Listen to tapes or video and express views about how a story or information has been presented<br>• Listen to and follow instructions accurately, asking for help and clarification if necessary. | | | Literacy 9 Creating and shaping texts | • Independently choose what to write about, plan and follow it through<br>• Use key features of narrative in their own writing<br>• Convey information and ideas in simple non-narrative forms<br>• Find and use new and interesting words and phrases, including story language<br>• Create short simple texts on paper and on screen that combine words with images (and sounds). |
| Literacy 3 Group discussion & interaction | • Take turns to speak, listen to others' suggestions and talk about what they are going to do<br>• Ask and answer questions, make relevant contributions, offer suggestions and take turns<br>• Explain their views to others in a small group, decide how to report the group's views to the class. | Literacy 7 Understanding and interpreting texts | • Identify the main events and characters in stories, and find specific information in simple texts<br>• Use syntax and context when reading for meaning<br>• Make predictions showing an understanding of ideas, events and characters<br>• Recognise the main elements that shape different texts<br>• Explore the effect of patterns of language and repeated words and phrases. | Literacy 10 Text structure and organisation | • Write chronological and non-chronological texts using simple structures<br>• Group written sentences together in chunks of meaning or subject. |
| Literacy 4 Drama | • Explore familiar themes and characters through improvisation and role-play<br>• Act out their own and well-known stories, using voices for characters<br>• Discuss why they like a performance. | | | Literacy 11 Sentence structure and punctuation | • Compose and write simple sentences independently to communicate meaning<br>• Use capital letters and full stops when punctuating simple sentences. |
| Literacy 5 Word recognition, coding and decoding | • Recognise and use alternative ways of pronouncing the graphemes already taught, for example, that the grapheme 'g' is pronounced differently in 'get' and 'gem'; the grapheme 'ow' is pronounced differently in 'how' and 'show'<br>• Recognise and use alternative ways of spelling the phonemes already taught, for example 'ae" can be spelt with 'ai', 'ay' or 'a-e'; begin to know which words contain which spelling alternatives.<br>• Identify the constituent parts of two-syllable and three-syllable words to support the application of phonic knowledge and skills. Recognise automatically an increasing number of familiar high frequency words | • Apply phonic knowledge and skills as the prime approach to reading and spelling unfamiliar words that are not completely decodable<br>• Read more challenging texts which can be decoded using their acquired phonic knowledge and skills; automatic recognition of high frequency words. Read and spell phonically decodable two-syllable and three-syllable words. | Literacy 12 Presentation | • Write most letters, correctly formed and orientated, using a comfortable and efficient pencil grip<br>• Write with spaces between words accurately<br>• Use the space bar and keyboard to type their name and simple texts. |

| | | | |
|---|---|---|---|
| **Literacy 1**<br>Speaking | • Speak with clarity and use appropriate intonation when reading and reciting texts<br>• Tell real and imagined stories using the conventions of familiar story language<br>• Explain ideas and processes using imaginative and adventurous vocabulary and nonverbal gestures to support communication | **Literacy 5**<br>Word recognition, coding and decoding | • Read independently and with increasing fluency longer and less familiar texts<br>• Spell with increasing accuracy and confidence, drawing on word recognition and knowledge of word structure, and spelling patterns<br>• Know how to tackle unfamiliar words that are not completely decodable<br>• Read and spell less common alternative graphemes including trigraphs<br>• Read high and medium frequency words independently and automatically |

## Literacy 1 — Speaking
- Speak with clarity and use appropriate intonation when reading and reciting texts
- Tell real and imagined stories using the conventions of familiar story language
- Explain ideas and processes using imaginative and adventurous vocabulary and nonverbal gestures to support communication

## Literacy 2 — Listening and responding
- Listen to others in class, ask relevant questions and follow instructions
- Listen to talk by an adult, remember some specific points and identify what they have learned
- Respond to presentations by describing characters, repeating some highlight and commenting constructively

## Literacy 3 — Group discussion and interaction
- Ensure that everyone contributes, allocate tasks, and consider alternatives and reach agreement
- Work effectively in groups by ensuring that each group member takes a turn challenging, supporting and moving on
- Listen to each other's views and preferences, agree the next steps to take and identify contributions by each group member

## Literacy 4 — Drama
- Adopt appropriate roles in small or large groups and consider alternative courses of action
- Present part of traditional stories, their own stories or work drawn from different parts of the curriculum for members of their own class
- Consider how mood and atmosphere are created in live or recorded performance

## Literacy 5 — Word recognition, coding and decoding
- Read independently and with increasing fluency longer and less familiar texts
- Spell with increasing accuracy and confidence, drawing on word recognition and knowledge of word structure, and spelling patterns
- Know how to tackle unfamiliar words that are not completely decodable
- Read and spell less common alternative graphemes including trigraphs
- Read high and medium frequency words independently and automatically

## Literacy 6 — Word structure and spelling
- Spell with increasing accuracy and confidence, drawing on word recognition and knowledge of word structure, and spelling patterns including common inflections and use of double letters
- Read and spell less common alternative graphemes including trigraphs

## Literacy 7 — Understanding and interpreting texts
- Draw together ideas and information from across a whole text, using simple signposts in the text
- Give reasons why things happen or characters change
- Explain organisational features of texts, including alphabetical order, layout, diagrams etc
- Use syntax and context to build their store of vocabulary when reading
- Explore how particular words are used, including words and expressions with similar meanings

## Literacy 8 — Engaging and responding to text
- Read whole books on their own, choosing and justifying selections
- Engage with books through exploring and enacting interpretations
- Explain their reactions to texts, commenting on important aspects

## Literacy 9 — Creating and shaping texts
- Draw on knowledge and experience of texts in deciding and planning what and how to write
- Sustain form in narrative, including use of person and time
- Maintain consistency in non-narrative, including purpose and tense
- Make adventurous word and language choices appropriate to the style and purpose of the text
- Select from different presentational features to suit particular writing purposes on paper and on screen

## Literacy 10 — Text structure and organisation
- Use planning to establish clear sections for writing
- Use appropriate language to make sections hang together

## Literacy 11 — Sentence structure and punctuation
- Write simple and compound sentences and begin to use subordination in relation to time and reason
- Compose sentences using tense consistently (present and past)
- Use question marks, and use commas to separate items in a list

## Literacy 12 — Presentation
- Write legibly, using upper and lower case letters appropriately within words, and observing correct spacing within and between words
- Form and use the four basic handwriting joins
- Word process short narrative and non-narrative texts

| Mathematics 1<br><br>Using and applying maths | • Solve problems involving counting, adding, subtracting, doubling or halving in the context of numbers, measures or money, for example to 'pay' and 'give change'<br><br>• Describe a puzzle or problem using numbers, practical materials and diagrams; use these to solve the problem and set the solution in the original context<br><br>• Answer a question by selecting and using suitable equipment, and sorting information, shapes or objects; display results using tables and pictures<br><br>• Describe simple patterns and relationships involving numbers or shapes; decide whether examples satisfy given conditions<br><br>• Describe ways of solving puzzles and problems, explaining choices and decisions orally or using pictures |
|---|---|
| Mathematics 2<br><br>Counting and understanding numbers | • Count reliably at least 20 objects, recognising that when rearranged the number of objects stays the same; estimate a number of objects that can be checked by counting<br><br>• Compare and order numbers, using the related vocabulary; use the equals (=) sign<br><br>• Read and write numerals from 0 to 20, then beyond; use knowledge of place value to position these numbers on a number track and number line<br><br>• Say the number that is 1 more or less than any given number, and 10 more or less for multiples of 10<br><br>• Use the vocabulary of halves and quarters in context |
| Mathematics 3<br><br>Knowing and using number facts | • Derive and recall all pairs of numbers with a total of 10 and addition facts for totals to at least 5; work out the corresponding subtraction facts<br><br>• Count on or back in ones, twos, fives and tens and use this knowledge to derive the multiples of 2, 5 and 10 to the tenth multiple<br><br>• Recall the doubles of all numbers to at least 10 |

| Mathematics 4<br><br>Calculating | • Relate addition to counting on; recognise that addition can be done in any order; use practical and informal written methods to support the addition of a one-digit number or a multiple of 10 to a one-digit or two- digit number<br><br>• Understand subtraction as 'take away' and find a 'difference' by counting up; use practical and informal written methods to support the subtraction of a one-digit number from a one-digit or two digit number and a multiple of 10 from a two- digit number<br><br>• Solve practical problems that involve combining groups of 2, 5 or 10, or sharing into equal groups<br><br>• Use the vocabulary related to addition and subtraction and symbols to describe and record addition and subtraction number sentences |
|---|---|
| Mathematics 5<br><br>Understanding shape | • Visualise and name common 2-D shapes and 3-D solids and describe their features; use them to make patterns, pictures and models<br><br>• Identify objects that turn about a point (e.g. scissors) or about a line (e.g. a door); recognise and make whole, half and quarter turns<br><br>• Visualise and use everyday language to describe the position of objects and direction and distance when moving them, for example when placing or moving objects on a game board |
| Mathematics 6<br><br>Measuring | • Estimate, measure, weigh and compare objects, choosing and using suitable uniform non-standard or standard units and measuring instruments (e.g. a lever balance, metre stick or measuring jug)<br><br>• Use vocabulary related to time; order days of the week and months; read the time to the hour and half hour |
| Mathematics 7<br><br>Handling data | • Answer a question by recording information in lists and tables; present outcomes using practical resources, pictures, block graphs or pictograms<br><br>• Use diagrams to sort objects into groups according to a given criterion; suggest a different criterion for grouping the same objects |

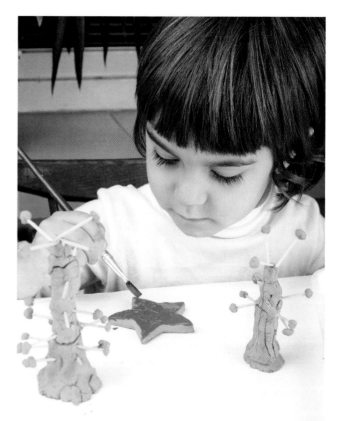

# KS1 Programme of Study (revised Framework objectives)    Mathematics - Year 2

## Mathematics 1
### Using and applying maths

- Solve problems involving addition, subtraction, multiplication or division in contexts of numbers, measures or pounds and pence
- Identify and record the information or calculation needed to solve a puzzle or problem; carry out the steps or calculations and check the solution in the context of the problem
- Follow a line of enquiry; answer questions by choosing and using suitable equipment and selecting, organising and presenting information in lists, tables and simple diagrams
- Describe patterns and relationships involving numbers or shapes, make predictions and test these with examples
- Present solutions to puzzles and problems in an organised way; explain decisions, methods and results in pictorial, spoken or written form, using mathematical language and number sentences

## Mathematics 2
### Counting and understanding numbers

- Read and write two-digit and three-digit numbers in figures and words; describe and extend number sequences and recognise odd and even numbers
- Count up to 100 objects by grouping them and counting in tens, fives or twos; explain what each digit in a two-digit number represents, including numbers where 0 is a place holder; partition two-digit numbers in different ways, including into multiples of 10 and 1
- Order two-digit numbers and position them on a number line; use the greater than (>) and less than (<) signs
- Estimate a number of objects; round two-digit numbers to the nearest 10
- Find one half, one quarter and three quarters of shapes and sets of objects

## Mathematics 3
### Knowing and using number facts

- Derive and recall all addition and subtraction facts for each number to at least 10, all pairs with totals to 20 and all pairs of multiples of 10 with totals up to 100
- Understand that halving is the inverse of doubling and derive and recall doubles of all numbers to 20, and the corresponding halves
- Derive and recall multiplication facts for the 2, 5 and 10 times-tables and the related division facts; recognise multiples of 2, 5 and 10
- Use knowledge of number facts and operations to estimate and check answers to calculations

## Mathematics 4
### Calculating

- Add or subtract mentally a one-digit number or a multiple of 10 to or from any two-digit number; use practical and informal written methods to add and subtract two-digit numbers
- Understand that subtraction is the inverse of addition and vice versa; use this to derive and record related addition and subtraction number sentences
- Represent repeated addition and arrays as multiplication, and sharing and repeated subtraction (grouping) as division; use practical and informal written methods and related vocabulary to support multiplication and division, including calculations with remainders
- Use the symbols +, -, ?, ÷ and = to record and interpret number sentences involving all four operations; calculate the value of an unknown in a number sentence (e.g. $\square \div 2 = 60$, $30 - \square = 24$).

## Mathematics 5
### Understanding shape

- Visualise common 2-D shapes and 3-D solids; identify shapes from pictures of them in different positions and orientations; sort, make and describe shapes, referring to their properties
- Identify reflective symmetry in patterns and 2-D shapes and draw lines of symmetry in shapes
- Follow and give instructions involving position, direction and movement
- Recognise and use whole, half and quarter turns, both clockwise and anticlockwise; know that a right angle represents a quarter turn

## Mathematics 6
### Measuring

- Estimate, compare & measure lengths, weights and capacities, choosing & using standard units (m, cm, kg, litre) & suitable measuring instruments
- Read the numbered divisions on a scale, and interpret the divisions between them (e.g. on a scale from 0 to 25 with intervals of 1 shown but only the divisions 0, 5, 10, 15 and 20 numbered); use a ruler to draw and measure lines to the nearest centimetre
- Use units of time (seconds, minutes, hours, days) and know the relationships between them; read the time to the quarter hour; identify time intervals, including those that cross the hour

## Mathematics 7
### Handling data

- Answer a question by collecting and recording data in lists and tables; represent the data as block graphs or pictograms to show results; use ICT to organise and present data
- Use lists, tables and diagrams to sort objects; explain choices using appropriate language, including 'not'

43

# KS1 Programme of Study for Key Stage 1: Science

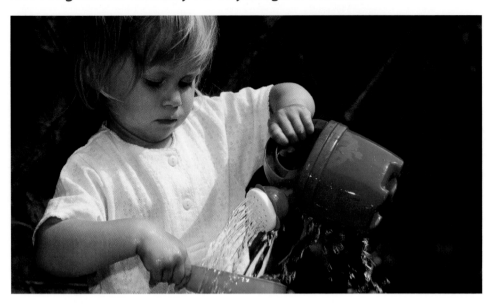

## SC1 Scientific enquiry

| Sc 1.1 | 1.1a | 1.1b | 1.1c | 1.1d |
|---|---|---|---|---|
| Planning | Ask questions 'How?', 'Why?', 'What if?' and decide how they might find answers to them | Use first-hand experience and simple information sources to answer questions | Think about what might happen before deciding what to do | Recognise when a test or comparison is unfair |
| **Sc 1.2** | **1.2a** | **1.2b** | **1.2c** | **1.2d** |
| Ideas and evidence, collecting evidence | Follow simple instructions to control the risks to themselves and to others | Explore using the senses of sight, hearing, smell, touch and taste as appropriate. Make and record observations and measurements | Communicate what happened in a variety of ways including using ICT | |
| **Sc 1.3** | **1.3a** | **1.3b** | **1.3c** | **1.3d** |
| Comparing evidence | Make simple comparisons (eg, hand span, shoe size) and identify simple patterns or associations, and try to explain it, drawing on their knowledge and understanding | Compare what happened with what they expected would happen and try to explain it. Draw on their knowledge and understanding | Review their work and explain what they did to others | |

## SC2 Life processes and living things

| Sc 2.1 | 2.1a | 2.1b | 2.1c | 2.1d |
|---|---|---|---|---|
| Life processes | Differences between things that are living and things that have never been alive | That animals, including humans, move, feed, grow, use their senses and reproduce | Relate life processes to animals and plants found in the local environment | |
| **Sc 2.2** | **2.2a** | **2.2b** | **2.2c** | **2.2d** |
| Ideas and evidence, collecting evidence | Recognise and compare the main external parts of the bodies of humans and other animals | That humans and other animals need food and water to stay alive | That taking exercise and eating the right types and amounts of food help humans to keep healthy | About the role of drugs as medicines |
| | **2.2e** | **2.2f** | **2.2g** | |
| | How to treat animals with care and sensitivity | That humans and other animals can produce off-spring and these off-spring grow into adults | About the senses that enable humans and other animals to be aware of the world around them | |
| **Sc 2.3** | **2.3a** | **2.3b** | **2.3c** | **2.3d** |
| Green plants | Recognise that plants need light and water to grow | To recognise and name the leaf, flowers, stem and root of flowering plants | That seeds grow into flowering plants | |
| **Sc 2.4** | **2.4a** | **2.4b** | | |
| Variation and classification | Recognise similarities and differences between themselves and others, and to treat others with sensitivity | Group living things according to observable similarities and differences | | |
| **Sc 2.5** | **2.5a** | **2.5b** | **2.5c** | |
| Living things in their environment | Find out about the different kinds of plants and animals in the local environment | Identify similarities & differences between local environments & ways in which these affect animals & plants that are found there | Care for the environment | |

## SC3 Materials and their properties

| Sc 3.1 Grouping materials | 3.1a | 3.1b | 3.1c | 3.1d |
|---|---|---|---|---|
| | Use their senses to explore and recognise the similarities and differences between materials | Sort objects into groups on the basis of their properties: texture, float, hardness and transparency and whether they are magnetic or non-magnetic | Recognise and name common types of material and recognise that some of them are found naturally | Find out about the uses of a variety of materials and how these are chosen for specific uses on the basis of their simple properties |

| Sc 3.2 Changing materials | 3.2a | 3.2b | | |
|---|---|---|---|---|
| | Find out how the shapes of objects made from some materials can be changed by some processes including squashing, bending, twisting and stretching | Explore and describe the way some everyday materials, e.g. water, chocolate, bread and clay, change when they are heated or cooled | | |

## SC4 Physical processes

| Sc 4.1 Electricity | 4.1a | 4.1b | 4.1c | 4.1d |
|---|---|---|---|---|
| | About everyday appliances that use electricity | Simple series circuits involving batteries, wires, bulbs and other components e.g. buzzers | How a switch can be used to break a circuit | Recognise when a test or comparison is unfair |

| Sc 4.2 Forces and motion | 4.2a | 4.2b | 4.2c | |
|---|---|---|---|---|
| | Find out about and describe the movement of familiar things e.g. cars going faster, slowing down, changing direction | That both pushes and pulls are examples of forces | To recognise that when things speed up, slow down, or change direction there is a cause | |

| Sc 4.3 Light and sound | 4.3a | 4.3b | 4.3c | 4.3d |
|---|---|---|---|---|
| | Identify different light sources including the sun | That darkness is the absence of light | That there are many kinds of sound and sources of sound | That sounds travel away from sources, getting fainter as they do so, and that they are heard |

# KS1 Programmes of Study

## History

| H 1 | 1a | 1b | 1c |
|---|---|---|---|
| Chronological understanding | Place events and objects in chronological order | Use common words and phrases relating to the passing of time e.g. before, after, a long time ago and past | Retrieve information that has been stored |
| **H 2** | **2a** | **2b** | |
| Knowledge & understanding of events people and changes | Recognise why people did things, why events happened and what happened as a result | Identify differences between ways of life at different times | |
| **H 3** | **3a** | | |
| Historical interpretation | Identify different ways in which the past is represented | | |
| **H 4** | **4a** | **4b** | |
| Historical enquiry | Find out about the past from a range of sources of information | Ask and answer questions about the past | |
| **H 5** | **5a** | | |
| Organisation and communication | Select from their knowledge of history and communicate it in a variety of ways | | |
| **H 6** | **6a** | **6b** | **6c** | **6d** |
| Breadth of study | Changes in their own lives and the way of life of their family or others around them | The way of life of people in the more distant past who lived in the local area or elsewhere in Britain | The lives of significant men, women or children | Past events from the history of Britain and the wider world |

## Design and Technology

| D&T 1 | 1a | 1b | 1c | 1d | 1e |
|---|---|---|---|---|---|
| Developing, planning and communicating ideas | Generate ideas by drawing on their own and other people's experiences | Develop ideas by hoping materials and putting together components | Talk about their ideas | Plan by suggesting what to do next as their ideas develop | Communicate ideas using a variety of materials including drawing and making moulds |
| **D&T 2** | **2a** | **2b** | **2c** | **2d** | **2e** |
| Working with tools, equipment and materials | Explore sensory qualities of materials | Measure, mark out, cut and shape | Assemble, join and combine materials | Use simple finishing techniques | Follow safe procedures |
| **D&T 3** | **3a** | **3b** | | | |
| Evaluating processes and products | Talk about their ideas | Identify improvements | | | |
| **D&T 4** | **4a** | **4b** | | | |
| Knowledge & understanding of materials and components | Working characteristics of materials | How mechanisms can be used | | | |
| **D&T 5** | **5a** | **5b** | **5c** | | |
| Breadth of study | Focused practical tasks | Design and make assignments | Investigate and evaluate products | | |

## Geography

| G 1.1 | 1.1a | 1.1b | 1.1c | 1.1d | |
|---|---|---|---|---|---|
| Geographical enquiry | Ask geographical questions | Observe and record | Express their own views about people, places, and environments | Communicate in different ways | |
| **G 1.2** | **1.2a** | **1.2b** | **1.2c** | **1.2d** | |
| Geographical skills | Use geographical vocabulary | Use fieldwork skills | Use globes, maps and plans at a range of scales | Use secondary sources of information | |
| **G 2** | **2a** | **2b** | **2c** | **2d** | **2e** |
| Knowledge and understanding of places | Identify and describe what places are like | Identify and describe what places are | Recognise how places become they way they are & how they are changing | Recognise how places compare with other places | Recognise how places are linked to other places in the world |
| **G 3** | **3a** | **3b** | **3c** | **3d** | |
| Knowledge & understanding of patterns & processes | Make observations about where things are located | Recognise changes in physical & human features | | | |
| **G 4** | **4a** | **4b** | | | |
| Knowledge & understanding of environment | Recognise changes in the environment | Recognise how the environment may be improved & sustained | | | |
| **G 5** | **5a** | **5b** | **5c** | **5d** | |
| Breadth of study | The locality of the school | A contrasting locality in the UK or overseas | Study at a local scale | Carry out fieldwork investigations outside the classroom | |

## ICT

| ICT 1.1 | 1.1a | 1.1b | 1.1c | 1.1d |
|---|---|---|---|---|
| Finding things out | Gather information from a variety of sources | Enter and store information in a variety of forms | Retrieve information that has been stored | |
| **ICT 1.2** | **1.2a** | **1.2b** | **1.2c** | **1.2d** |
| Developing ideas and making things happen | Use text, tables, images and sound to develop their ideas | Select from and add to information thay have rerieved for particular purposes | Plan and give instructions to make things happen | Try things out and explore what happens in real and imaginary instructions |
| **ICT 2** | **2a** | **2b** | | |
| Exchanging and sharing information | Share their ideas by presenting information in a variety of forms | Present their completed work effectively | | |

## Physical Education

| PE 1 | 1a | 1b | |
|---|---|---|---|
| Aquiring and developing skills | Explore basic skills, actions and ideas with increasing understanding | Remember and repeat simple skills & actions with increasing control | |
| **PE 2** | **2a** | **2b** | **2c** |
| Selecting and applying skills, tactics and compositional ideas | Explore how to choose and apply skills and actions in sequence & in combination | Vary the way they perform skills by using simple tactics and movement phrases | Apply rules and conventions for different activities |
| **PE 3** | **3a** | **3b** | **3c** |
| Evaluating and improving performance | Describe what they have done | Observe, describe & copy what others have done | Use what they have learnt to improve the quality and control of their work |
| **PE 4** | **4a** | **4b** | |
| Knowledge and understanding of fitness and health | How important it is to be active | Recognise and describe how their bodies feel during different activities | |
| **PE 5** | **5a** | **5b** | **5c** |
| Breadth of study | Dance | Games | Gymnastics |

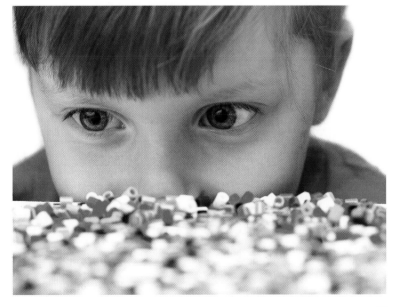

## Art and Design

| A&D 1 | 1a | 1b | | |
|---|---|---|---|---|
| Exploring and developing ideas | Record from first hand observation, experience & imagination | Ask and answer questions about the starting points for their work | | |
| **A&D 2** | **2a** | **2b** | **2c** | |
| Investigating and making art, craft and design | Investigate the possibilities of materials and processes | Try out tools and techniques and apply these | Represent observations, ideas and feelings | |
| **A&D 3** | **3a** | **3b** | | |
| Evaluating and developing work | Review what they and others have done | Identify what they might change | | |
| **A&D 4** | **4a** | **4b** | **4c** | |
| Knowledge and understanding of materials and components | Visual and tactile elements | Materials and processes used in making art, craft and design | Differences and similarities in the work of artists, craftspeople and designers | |
| **A&D 5** | **5a** | **5b** | **5c** | **5d** |
| Breadth of study | Exploring a range of starting points | Working on their own and collaborating with others | Using a range of materials and processes | Investigating different types of art, craft and design |

## Music

| M 1 | 1a | 1b | 1c | |
|---|---|---|---|---|
| Performing skills | Use their voices expressively by singing songs, chants, rhymes | Play tuned and untuned instruments | Rehearse and perform with others | |
| **M 2** | **2a** | **2b** | | |
| Composing skills | Create musical patterns | Explore, choose and organise sounds and musical ideas | | |
| **M 3** | **3a** | **3b** | | |
| Responding and reviewing — appraising skills | Explore and express their ideas and feelings about music | Make improvements to their own work | | |
| **M 4** | **4a** | **4b** | **4c** | |
| Responding and reviewing — listening skills | Listen with concentration and internalise & recall sounds | How combined musical elements can be organised | How sounds can be made in different ways | |
| **M 5** | **5a** | **5b** | **5c** | **5d** |
| Breadth of study | A range of musical activities | Responding to a range of starting points | Working on their own, in groups and as a class | A range of live and recorded music |

## PSHE

| PSHE 1 | 1a | 1b | 1c | 1d | 1e | | | |
|---|---|---|---|---|---|---|---|---|
| Developing confidence & responsibility & making the most of their abilities | Recognise their likes and dislikes, what is fair and unfair, what is right and wrong | Share their opinions on things that matter to them and their views | Recognise, name and deal with their feelings in a positive way | Think about themselves, learn from their experiences and recognise what they are good at | How to set simple goals | | | |
| **PSHE 2** | **2a** | **2b** | **2c** | **2d** | **2e** | **2f** | **2g** | |
| Preparing to play an active role as citizens | Take part in discussions with one other person and the whole class | Take part in a simple debate about topical issues | Recognise choices they make, and the difference between right and wrong | Realise that people and other living things have needs, and that they have responsibilities to meet them | That they belong to various groups and communities, such as a family | What improves and harms their local, natural & built environments | Contribute to the life of the class and school | Realise that money comes from different sources |
| **PSHE 3** | **3a** | **3b** | **3c** | **3d** | **3e** | **3f** | **3g** | |
| Developing a healthier lifestyle | Make simple choices that improve their health and wellbeing | Maintain personal hygiene | How some diseases spread and can be controlled | About the process of growing from young to old and how people's needs change | Name the main parts of the body | That household products and medicines can be harmful | Rules for, and ways of, keeping safe, basic road safety | |
| **PSHE 4** | **4a** | **4b** | **4c** | **4d** | **4e** | | | |
| Developing good relationships and respecting differences | Recognise how their behaviour affects other people | Listen to other people and play and work co-operatively | Identify and respect differences and similarities between people | That family and friends should care for each other | That there are different types of teasing and bullying, that bullying is wrong | | | |

**PSHE: non-statutory guidance**